Reframing Negative Thinking

*Transform Your Perspective, Calm
Your Mind, Find Peace.*

Zera Young

Your Free Gift

· *Learn to recognize your limiting beliefs*
· *Get easy-to-apply techniques to create positive beliefs*
· *Start your journey towards a calm and peaceful life!*

To get instant access visit:
zerayoung.com
or use the following QR-code:

If you want to achieve anything you want, make
sure to grab the free book.

Contents

Introduction

When people ask me why I decided to write this book, they expect me to say that it's because of my expertise. In reality, I was just inspired to create something that will help people get out of their own way. I see kids in middle school or high school, already succumbing to the throes of negativity. In colleges and universities around the globe, we are seeing more and more young adults feeling lost, discouraged, and pessimistic about their futures. Later in life, these students grow into unhappy adults—stuck in a boring job and not even seeing the point of trying to escape. To them, it seems as if only the lucky ones become successful while the rest of us are forced deal with the innumerous adversities of life.

Seeing so many young people not able to tap into their potential all because of the way their mind is wired, is what pushed me to create this book.

I have been divorced for nearly a decade now. I'm not going to lie to you, that period of my life was tough; I experienced a sense of loss, sadness, and grief, just like most other divorcees. What I realized through those emotions, however, was that I remained myself. I expected myself to shut down at some point, finding it unbearable to move on. To my pleasant surprise that expectation never came true. In fact, I soon found myself learning the difference between the feelings I was experiencing and the wonderful potential I had in my future; the people I had yet to meet and love, the countries I had yet to see and the languages I had yet to learn. My sadness didn't consume my being. I felt it, as you do with any loss, but it was separate from who I was. I looked forward to changing and experiencing my life in a whole new way. I had never felt more powerful in my life than at that moment. From this feeling sprouted my inspiration to help others feel this way.

Throughout my life, I used to be quite an influenceable person—I generally credit this to my previous people-pleasing tendency. As a child and teenager, I remember trying to conform to every new friend I made. Instead of finding who I was, I let others decide. Sad, isn't it? Even throughout college, I struggled to feel comfortable with myself. Between my family, friends, partners, and coworkers, I must have seemed like a different person to each. Through these types of attachments, I became vulnerable to their mindsets. I remember a particular boyfriend who made my life nearly unbearable—not because he was an abusive partner or anything, but rather because his constant pessimism rubbed off on me. I stopped setting high goals for myself, taking on challenges, and exploring myself. We both were lumps of disappointment. For over a year, I felt miserable while being unaware of the reason. Slowly, I began to notice that when I would take trips with my friends away from my then-boyfriend, I felt different. At first, I was confused. After all, we were supportive of each other, and if I ever felt bad about something or myself, he was there for me. Yet, here I was, watching myself put my own spark out. Eventually, I realized that the support we were offering each other was only confirming our disappointment in the world. We listened, talked, discussed, but failed to uplift each other. We fed into loops of negativity that only further reinforced our beliefs that the world was a bad place where bad things were bound to happen. Within a month or two after coming to that conclusion, I found a way to respectfully end things and saw the difference that being alone made.

Through single life, boyfriends, and ex-husbands, I have seen it all. I realize now that having good people around you is important, but nothing will ever top being good to yourself. We will feel alone at times, no matter how hard we try not to. It is how we handle being by ourselves that can show us the true measure of our relationship with ourselves. Are we kind to ourselves? Do we put too much pressure on ourselves? Do we belittle our accomplishments?

There are many, many ways one can make life hell for themselves. Sadly, this is a natural route for a large majority of the population. Without unlearning these things, we will stay harmful toward ourselves and potentially others.

I've always believed that the world had too much to offer for so many people to not let themselves experience it. Word by word, I want to help you and anyone else who comes across this book to take the power back from negativity—and not through commonly overused phrases mask your sadness. You can do this through advice that will actually change your life bit by bit.

"You don't have it that bad!"

"You should be grateful for what you've got."

"Just change your mindset—be positive!"

We've all heard this so-called advice. However, no one seems to explain *how* we should accomplish these things. Psychology and mindset are extremely complex issues. They have to do with emotions, neurology, physical lifestyle, and life history. That's why it's so hard to come up with a solution that can work for everyone. So, instead of doing that, I will be providing you with extremely applicable basics of transforming your negative thoughts into more constructive ones. There is no one-size-fits-all, but there are different options available.

Chapter 1
Understanding Negative Thinking

"Dwelling on the negative simply contributes to its power"

— Shirley MacLaine

The first thing you need to know is that your brain is technically wired to think negatively. Originally, this wiring served as a defense mechanism—one that dates back to the dawn of mankind, when people were cavemen and cavewomen with only a few main objectives: hunt and scavenge for food and protect themselves, and their offspring, from danger. If you think the world is a dangerous place now, imagine what it was like back then, with none of the amenities or safety measures we have today. The average caveman had to be wary of savage beasts and, well, savage fellow cavemen. Nowadays, modern society is practically built on businesses that have found a way to simplify and make life more pleasant. As if restaurants were not good enough of an idea, we now have food delivery services. The objectives of an average person are now multiplied. With safety and food accounted for (for the most part), we now busy ourselves with other things. We worry about promotions and learning to play an instrument and being environmentally friendly.

Again, this was not what people worried about in the past. With food and safety being their primary concerns, the brains of primitive humans began accommodating these needs. Their brains learned to be extra aware of the numerous dangers that posed a threat to their lives, and their negative appreciation of said dangers is what kept them alive.

Although most of these dangers are no longer as prevalent in the contemporary age, that negative thought mechanism has managed to persist, being handed down from generation to generation, like getting an inheritance that is more of a burden than a gift. At least, that is how we perceive it now, right? But what if we started seeing it as a gift once again; a gift that we often mismanage and fail to have control over, but a gift nonetheless. Negative thoughts are meant to serve a purpose. It is through a lack of knowledge and experience we fail to see them for the beneficial tendencies they are. In reality, negative thoughts continue to be useful for us—and often life-saving.

For early humans, assuming something unfamiliar is life-threatening could determine whether they lived or died. If they came across an unfamiliar berry, they would be risking their offspring's lives if they assumed it was harmless and fed it to them. Instead, these people would have assumed the worst and decided their course of action from there. Nowadays, we apply a similar logic, but to much less drastic situations. We might be afraid of asking someone out, thinking that they'll reject us immediately and we'll never recover. Similar assumptions, right? Yet, one seemed to protect the person, while the other kept them from taking an innocent risk. With examples like these, it becomes quite clear that negativity is not the villain we make it out to be. Rather, we just have the responsibility of learning how to use and apply it.

Our Place in the Modern World

There seems to have been more than one pandemic in recent history. One involves a life-threatening virus that has traveled around the globe, while the other is found in people's mindsets. One can argue that living in the Paleolithic era of humanity, hunting and scavenging for food is the worst life imaginable. This is probably true for most people who enjoy sleeping in a nice bed, taking hot showers, and exchanging currency for prepared foods and other ingredients. However, in a lot of ways, one might romanticize the simplicity of the past; not necessarily the dawn of humanity, but let's say a few hundred years back. Nowadays, we seem to be faced with a new type of technology every few months, falling behind on trends, and never having time to do everything we want. The world has been far from perfect, with the present included. Modern society has its fair share of wonderful additions, while, in turn, making other aspects of our lives pay for them.

In my everyday life, I come across so many people who are lost. They don't know why they're doing what they're doing or even whether they want to be doing it at all. As many as 44% of undergraduate students don't know what they want to be doing after they graduate from university (Concrete, 2022). Of course, some people's reactions might be disbelief, while others may blame these students for being so out of touch with their desires. But is it really their fault?

In most countries around the world, students are asked to pick a field of study, in which they will have to invest a lot of money, at the young age of 18. A few lucky ones might know what they want to study, while the rest are left struggling to make such a crucial choice. If they choose 'wrong', they may end up spending years of their young lives and thousands of dollars on an education they neither needed nor desired. So, many begin to contemplate this choice based on factors other than true desire, including: how much money they can make from this degree, how hard it is to get into the program, and how the people around them will perceive them with such a degree. Even without a true calling for their choice of program, they might carry on studying it for years, getting a degree, and even becoming a professional in that field before realizing their life doesn't truly belong to them. Being in your 30s, 40s, or even older, and realizing that you've been living a life based on somebody else's criteria is a terrifying realization but not an uncommon one. For many reasons, these poor students are not to blame. Instead, the root of the issue lies in the way our society is organized and the immense pressure that is put upon the shoulders of these young adults.

A similar phenomenon follows us into later adulthood, where the same concept is applied: we make lifestyle choices that we *think* will make us happy based on someone else's standards. Hustle culture is a fantastic example of a modern mindset that has managed to decrease the quality of life for millions of people, while pretending to do quite the opposite. If you aren't already familiar with this term, hustle culture can be defined as the belief that true happiness and success come to those who spend as much time as possible being productive and earning money. Not only does this philosophical trend leave no time for rest for the affected individuals, but its true benefit is not to the individual—it's to capitalism. We have somehow managed to convince ourselves that overworking our bodies and minds like some lab rats is the true definition of prosperity.

In many cultures and religions around the world, the idea of hustle culture would be laughed at. Thanks to many Eastern beliefs that emphasize the importance of balance and calmness, this phenomenon would not have made it past the fame of a niche Facebook group. And yet, here so many of us are acting as if working for 90 hours per week is something worth bragging about. Why do we use our exhaustion as a measure of social status? Too many of us fail to listen to ourselves, and instead take advice from people who may not have our best interests in mind.

Negativity: A Cultural Phenomenon?

Let's take a look around the world: How do different countries' and cultures' happiness levels compare? Well, some of you may or may not be surprised to know that Nordic countries are among the happiest in the world. In 2019, Finland scored highest on happiest, followed by Denmark, Norway, Iceland, and eventually Sweden in seventh place (Bloom, 2022). Their taxes are higher than in the United States, for example, yet the average Finn is much happier than the average American. Not surprisingly, Nordic countries also tend to score highest in quality of life; this pertains to education, social welfare, healthcare, access to necessities, etcetera. Just to mention a few wonderful differences, these countries have strict laws that guarantee adequate maternal and paternal leave, a humane prison system focused on rehabilitation, and tax distribution that allows citizens to trust their social security. Unfortunately, the same can rarely be said for much of the United States, where happiness has been *declining*. Prices in the US are rising exponentially while income is not—can this be the reason we're so unhappy? The statistical comparison of quality of life and happiness between North America and Northern Europe sure seems to suggest so, but it isn't the *only* reason.

Ikigai Is Key

In Japan, there exists an ancient philosophy called Ikigai. Ikigai is often regarded as a source of someone's life purpose or reason for living. This philosophy and way of life is often used as part of the reason why people living in the blue zone of Okinawa Japan have such a high life expectancy. A National Geographic explorer, Dan Buettner, recorded a stone inscription he found in Okinawa, Japan—"At 80, you are merely a youth. At 90, if your ancestors invite you into heaven, ask them to wait until you are 100—then, you might consider it" (Goss, 2020). In the entire world, there are currently five identified blue zones in which people are living the longest and are generally very healthy. These zones have been the subject of many scientific and philosophical studies, and the insights provided by their citizens can teach the rest of us a lot.

Okinawans have commonly suggested the following factors of their lives as the reasons for their health and longevity:

- **Having a sense of purpose.** As I described at the beginning of this chapter, our fast-paced lives in the West often shift our focus from purpose to productivity. We fail to ask ourselves: What is the point of productivity if it has no purpose? Among other populations, work-life balance is not treated as an afterthought, but rather, as a priority. Through Ikigai, people make finding their purpose a central focus of their time because they believe this is what grants them their good health and long lives. The practice of developing a sense of purpose has a lot to do with *why* we feel our emotions and not just *what* we are feeling. This demands a lot of introspection and resistance to shying away from what you might uncover when you examine yourself more deeply.

- **Deep focus and dedication.** As said, Ikigai adds purpose to people's actions. This, in turn, gives them the ability to focus on their tasks with much more ease than the average person. Knowing that what they are tasked with doing is benefitting their life's purpose, they have no problem mustering up enough concentration that would shock the average, Western procrastinator. Developing focus on things that matter is said to be a crucial aspect of improving your relationship with your life's purpose. To do so, I would recommend starting slow; challenge yourself to work on something you've been putting off for 15 to 30 minutes per day. If it's something that has any value to you, you will start to notice that this allotted time becomes easier and easier to stick to.

The true challenge of improving your focus is to trust yourself enough to start.

- **Maintaining physical health.** In Okinawa, the key to longevity stems beyond purpose and focus. In fact, many Okinawans emphasize the crucial relationship between physical and mental health. Without physical health it is difficult to maintain good mental health, and without proper mental health it is difficult to stick to healthy eating and exercise regimens. We often associate diet and exercise with losing weight or building muscle mass, but its effects envelop much more of the human body. Neurologically, our brains have been found to release feel-good hormones following a workout that are capable of uplifting our moods for up to 24 hours afterward. Not surprisingly, staying active daily is a commitment many Okinawans partake in. They also report following the 80% rule—only eating until you feel 80% full to avoid being drained by overeating. A lot of Okinawans eat a largely vegetable-based diet with only a few meat products, if any at all.

- **Having a strong, supportive network.** The term "moai" refers to a dedicated friend group that supports one another for nearly an entire lifetime. It is this social network that provides people with adequate socialization, authentic companionship, and the option to receive true emotional and mental support. These aspects are important to everyone's emotional processing, and positively impact the way we manage difficult situations and feelings. Through moai, Okinawans receive all of these great benefits that help them stay mentally and emotionally satisfied. Now, like most people, you may not get to experience the stability of a moai, but the underlying lesson is that having people you can lean on from time to time isn't something to overlook; it truly improves your quality of life.

The Dark Side of Technology

Social media is complicated. I'm not one to bash the progress that we have made with technology, but I am one to notice its flaws. Social media was initially made to facilitate our interactions with people all around the globe. This made travel and moving away much easier for billions of people and was, put simply, a great invention. However, the dark side of social media did not wait long to manifest. As humans, it is normal for us to feel proud of ourselves. Furthermore, we want *others* to confirm this feeling and be proud of us as well. Many people believe that the need for external validation is a bad thing, but it isn't; it's a normal desire, and we can never truly get rid of every ounce of it. But, scrolling through social media we see a very different end of this spectrum. We come across dozens, hundreds, if not thousands of posts per week whose *only* purpose is external validation. There is no getting around it: social media can easily make a person feel bad about themselves or their life if they give it the power to do so. Seeing extravagant vacations, five-star dinners, and cars that cost as much as our houses will unavoidably have a negative effect on our mindset. Suddenly, the life we might have been satisfied with previously seems like nothing in comparison to the glamorous glimpses we see of other people.

Comparison is a dangerous tendency of ours. Just like nega-tivity, comparison has beneficial roots. In other words, it benefitted us as cavepeople in a similar fashion: If you saw a fellow caveman get three times as many berries as you, your tendency to compare would probably push you to find out how they managed to do so. However, when the things we begin comparing become superficial or simply luxurious, our reactions brew toxicity. Not only do we become vulner-able to jealousy, envy, and hostility, our gratitude for what we *do* have automatically decreases—and suddenly, nothing is enough.

Rejecting the Herd

There's a contradiction in Western society that contributes to our happiness, or lack thereof. Unlike many cultures found in the Eastern parts of the world, our society is very individualistic rather than collectivist; meaning, we each tend to focus on our independence more than on the inter-connectivity of society. Some even find this tendency to be a little cold to others, breeding a lack of trust within the popu-lation. However, even with all this individuality, we still often struggle to take our own paths.

When someone chooses to be themselves—in whatever capacity that may be—it is still regarded as a brave choice. This leads us to the discovery that individuality in modern society is solely about independence rather than an embrace of uniqueness; you get rewarded for not depending on others, but still punished for challenging the standards set by society.

Although there has been a slight decrease in this in the past decade or so, the choice many young adults make to not go to college, for example, is still regarded as a bad one. With insurmountable university fees, this choice seems like a no-brainer to many people. But, to society, this choice is not a celebrated one. You have to be strong in order to make a choice that doesn't make most people happy, even if it only affects you. No wonder that with this psychology, so many people simply make choices to appease others.

The Effects of Negativity

If I were to ask each reader of this book to create a pros and cons list of negativity, I would expect to see a disequilibrium between the two; most people see negativity as a thing they want to get rid of.

The benefits of negativity are certainly present but get overshadowed by the innumerous drawbacks. For example, negativity can prevent us from getting hurt by something in the future, such as getting rejected from a job we wanted. On the other hand, the same negativity can prevent us from getting exactly what we want in the future, such as being hired for that job we really wanted. Our negativity is a double-edged sword, and we act according to which side we think we will regret the least. Most people in society are risk-averse, meaning they prefer to take smaller risks and as infrequently as possible. This group is most likely to not apply for their dream job at all because they believe the possibility of rejection is not worth the possibility of acceptance. Why is that?

An interesting psychological phenomenon explains why. People are notoriously bad at predicting our future emotional reactions. We overestimate both potential happiness and potential sadness. For instance, imagine how you would feel about getting your dream car or house. In your mind, you are likely to think your life will feel just a little more complete and that the happiness from this purchase will fill many voids, in turn increasing your life's overall quality. However, in reality, the happiness from such a purchase tends to wear off pretty quickly and completely fails to satisfy the buyer long-term. The same is applied to situations of sadness; we will predict that being rejected from a job will crush us and demotivate us for a very long time, which is simply not true. Much like the happiness from a luxurious purchase, the sadness from an event wears off as well. This phenomenon is called *impact bias* and is relevant to most people. Winning the lottery doesn't mean lifelong happiness just as much as experiencing an unfortunate accident doesn't mean lifelong sadness. Convincing ourselves otherwise leads to dissatisfaction and only brews more negativity.

As true as it is that negativity also brings benefits, let's focus on why you don't want too much of it. After all, why else would you be reading this book? So, to examine why reframing negative thinking is an unavoidable task for happiness, let's take a look at what life would look like if you didn't.

Self-Esteem and Confidence

Negativity provides easy access to answering the unknown. What I mean by this, is that it offers us an idea of how something might turn out, and therefore becomes easy to overuse. Rather than wonder how we might look in a certain outfit, negativity allows us to find an answer: bad. Clearly, the downside to having the answer is that that answer will fail to be positive.

When there is too much negativity, it starts applying itself to everything—your career, your appearance, your skills, the outcomes of your risks, etcetera. Self-esteem and confidence are no exceptions, either. Someone with too much negativity will inevitably focus on the bad of something more than they realize the good of it. This also applies to themselves. They will often underestimate their skills and overestimate their flaws. While walking through a crowded place, they might feel exceptionally self-conscious regarding a small issue with their wardrobe that others will likely not even notice. Negativity causes them to pick and pick at themselves until they feel unworthy of success.

This low self-esteem and low confidence consequently cause a decrease in motivation. If everything will fail, what's the point of even trying? The person slowly becomes more and more risk-averse until taking chances doesn't seem worth it whatsoever. If they don't break out of this mindset, it soon consumes all their potential. Their dreams, their goals, their desire—all of these will be no match to the scary potential outcomes that negativity has spewed out. These things will not be sought after, making them irrelevant to the individual's life.

Avoiding this outcome requires either luck or effort. Either you're lucky enough to never get sucked into this vortex in the first place or you make a commitment to actively fight against it. Your mind is more powerful than the things that influence it. Negativity is not your whole mind; it is simply a mindset—and the great thing about mindsets is that they can definitely be changed.

Key Points

Let's look over the most important takeaways from Chapter 1:

- Negativity is not innately bad and can be quite beneficial
- Negativity in the modern world has become overwhelming
- Our perception of the world is influenced by our environment
- Ikigai teaches the importance of finding purpose
- Choosing to reject society's influence of negativity is a radical step
- Too much negativity affects your life and your perception of yourself

Chapter 2
Psychology and Philosophy Over the Years

"History is the interpretation of the significance that the past has for us."

— Johan Huizinga

The quote above will make sense in a moment, as in the chapter, we are learning from our past as a society. But first, let me tell you why this is significant. When I first got divorced, I jotted down a list of things I was eager to finally do. It's not like I couldn't have done them while I was still married, but something felt as if it was holding me back—until I got divorced. I used to be 'smarter' about my money. I think I was even a little too cautious. At one point I may have forgotten that money is meant to be spent, yet all the while I saved for a house and car that were still years away on my timeline. When I became single once again, I eventually dedicated a good part of my paycheck to travel. One year I went to South America, another I visited some countries in Asia, then I went to see a college friend in Northern Europe—these were truly revitalizing experiences, one after another. In all honesty, I have no intention of stopping. I have found what makes me appreciate my life and I will not apologize for enjoying it as much as I do.

The purpose of these trips, however, does not meet its end on my Instagram feed. Yes, I do it largely for the thrill it gives me, but I take home much more than a few pretty pictures and a souvenir. Thanks to my various adventures, I have learned more from them than I did from the first 35 years of my life.

Following my divorce, the first place I traveled to was Brazil. I had a friend in my late 20s who was infatuated with this country and later met a serious boyfriend there. She kept inviting me to go with her on her trips, but I often found excuses not to—I was intimidated. With my divorce came my newfound sense of adventure, and that intimidation disappeared.

When I got to Brazil, I understood why she fell in love with it. She was an attractive person, not just physically, but energetically; Brazil reflected these characteristics just the same. I have never been too much into the party scene and was quite cautious when it came to the Amazon Rainforest, so I spent my time exploring the culture. I visited museum after museum, as well as many landmarks, and lots of other things you could find on the first two pages of Yelp suggestions. My trip didn't end there, however, as I found myself in Peru next. Here, the most popular destination is evidently the famous Machu Picchu; but, even after visiting such exquisite sites, I didn't feel fully satisfied.

Fast forward a few weeks and I was finally comfortable. Or rather, I was comfortable being uncomfortable. I was still equally nervous striking up conversations with random people, but I managed to stop looking at Yelp and began interacting with the locals as best as I could (Google Translate certainly helped). Every city and country I visited afterward, I did the same—I started being less interested in the tourist attractions and more focused on learning from the people. I could tell countless stories and recount endless conversations that have all shaped me into who I am today, but all I will say is this: There is so much we do not know.

Only through dozens, if not hundreds, of people had I learned so much. They told me stories of their families and traditions, invited me to dinner, showed me around neighborhoods, and so much more that opened my eyes to ways of life I had never even considered. It is from these interactions that I realized how crucial broadening our knowledge is; not just about facts and statistics, but about people and cultures.

Negativity is born from many things. Some are environmental, and some are from repeated choices, but the trends indicating that some cultures tend to be happier than others are not a coincidence. It is my solid belief that learning how philosophies and ways of life fluctuate between cultures and time periods can make it so much easier for us to change our perspectives. If you are truly interested in creating a mindset for yourself that will benefit your success, I can only recommend you have a basic knowledge of this information. In fact, by seeing the changes in mindset that occur throughout the world's history makes us realize that standards change. If you don't like the mentality that has been cultivated around you, you don't have any obligation to follow it.

Ancient Times

Even without doing any research, most people are probably aware of how drastically the world has changed over the past few thousand years. This change has not only regarded technology and medicine, but even just the way we tend to think. Witnessing someone being burned at the stake or decapitated in public is an unthinkable event nowadays, but in the past it might have been a fun Friday night for some people. This level of violence is insane to think about for us, but back then it was not something most people were extremely affected by. Were they simply born with characteristics that better equipped them for this lifestyle or were they influenced by their environments? How about surgeons or soldiers, even in the modern day? Some people I know would rather break an arm than get poked with a needle, while others spend 50+ hours a week cutting people open. There must be some aspects of this that are innate, while others are certainly products of the way we grow up.

A lot of people associate the far past with violence, pain, war, and so on. Most of us can't even imagine living 100 years ago, let alone 500 or 2,000. However, I'd argue that this completely overlooks the wonderful things that arose during that time. In fact, in a lot of ways, life back then was a lot more peaceful.

The Influence of Hinduism and Buddhism

Two years after my South American trip, I finally made it to Asia. I had been once before to Japan as a young teenager, accompanying my father on a brief business trip, and I had been longing to go back ever since. Fast forward 20-something years and I finally got to go again.

I probably don't have to tell you that Asia and its multitude of diverse cultures is an absolute gem. No, I don't mean the Asia that some people in the West may just assume refers to China, Japan, and Korea. I mean the Asia that also includes rural Thailand, the beaches of Indonesia, gorgeous Indian markets, and countless other countries. We often limit our knowledge of a place and time to what we are shown. In the West, most of Asian culture that we have access to comes from East Asia, which is why people's knowledge beyond China, Japan, and Korea tends to be quite restricted. But what if we ventured beyond those?

During my trip to Asia as an adult, I visited several countries. For the relevance of this chapter, however, I will focus on India. This wonderful Southeast Asian country has so much to offer, I'd need ten books the size of this one to even scratch the surface of what I've learned. Its rich culture and history have some of the oldest origins known to man, with several religions making up the bulk of its population's beliefs.

Hinduism is one of the oldest religions that we are aware of. In fact, when the Hindu *Vedas* (collections of religious texts) were written between 1500 and 1200 BCE, Hinduism had already existed for quite some time. The religion has existed for more than 3,500 years and remains relevant in today's world, with over 1 billion followers globally. So, what about this religion is continuing to attract so many people?

Hinduism has a main objective: escape *samsara*—the cycle of death and rebirth—through the accumulation of good *karma*—the energy of a person's past actions. This objective is called *moksha*. In this religion, there exists an ultimate, supreme being that is often referred to as Brahman. Oftentimes, this being is represented by hundreds of different deities. The appearance of so many gods and goddesses often leads people to think of Hinduism as a polytheistic religion, but that tends to be misrepresented.

Unlike Hinduism, Buddhism is slightly newer and does not have a supreme being, but did also originate in India. Around 500 BCE, a man named Siddartha Guatama (later known as the Buddha) first reached enlightenment. Buddhism has several overlaps with Hinduism—it also possesses the main objective of escaping reincarnation, which is also called samsara. This is also accelerated through the buildup of good karma, however, there is a better way of doing so. In Buddhism, there exists the concept of *nirvana* or spiritual enlightenment that connects the individual so strongly to the other realm that they don't need to be reincarnated again. Similarly to Hinduism, Buddhism continues to interest a lot of people around the world and currently has around 500 million followers.

The reason I gave you a quick overview of these religions is to introduce you to something I found particularly interesting while learning about Buddhism: In this particular belief system, Buddhists are urged to follow the *Middle Way*. This concept teaches the importance of balance. Instead of trying to reach a state of enlightenment through having too much or too little, people should strive to have just enough balance for a comfortable life, but not anything of excess. Why I found this so interesting is because several other religions often believe that worldly possessions are vain because our spirits and/or souls don't need them. I found a connection between the concept of the Middle Way and the approach I used to maintain my mental health in good condition. Too much of something can be as bad as too little of something, and vice versa—and this applies to negativity.

Mindfulness From Zen Buddhism

A branch of Buddhism called Zen Buddhism happens to focus on a person's mindset and lifestyle. It centers around the cultivation of peace and calmness, not only through one's thinking, but by changing their surroundings to facilitate this process. This is also something that I have found useful for my own life: The way we live, the habits we form, and the actions we make all contribute to forming our mindsets. Buddhism, Hinduism, and particularly Zen Buddhism, all promote mindfulness.

Mindfulness is a state of mind that is meant to make us aware of our present. It is often applied to all areas of life, including how we eat, how we focus, what we say, etcetera. Mindful eating is a popular approach to cultivating a healthy diet, through attentiveness. This would look like paying special attention to what you are consuming: how does it taste? What are its colors? How would you describe the texture?

Mindfulness is believed to promote a calm mind—one in which there are no obstacles to enjoying the moment. Rather than focusing on stressing about the future or regretting the past, mindfulness brings us to this very moment; it quiets the mind and allows us to stop being influenced by pestering thoughts. This might be one of the best ways to stop letting negativity take over.

15th to 19th Centuries

It's quite impossible to capture all of the cultural changes that occurred around the world in five whole centuries that may have influenced the population's mindset, but we can focus on important trends. When we look at the way people's approaches to life have changed from the 15th to 19th centuries, we are making a big generalization. After all, there were always outliers and major differences between different places in the world, making it difficult to find a common average.

As we look at the overview of each era, we begin to realize the patterns. Oftentimes, we can directly see a connection between societal standards and expectations, and the mindset people had at that time.

Renaissance Era

The Renaissance Era lasted between the 14th and 17th centuries. Unlike the Middle Ages, which came directly before—often characterized as dark and centered largely around survival from various dangers—the Renaissance Era is known for promoting classical art, music, and philosophy. Suddenly, the world became a little less dark with a lot more beauty. This era produced some of the most famous and intricate works of art and music. The word "renaissance" even means "rebirth" in French, symbolizing this colossal transformation in the Western European world.

One huge product of the Renaissance Era is humanism—a strong intellectual movement that encouraged people to focus on being human. Rather than doing everything out of a religious or survival need, humanism brought to light the importance of savoring our lives. This, in turn, was captured in the impressive works of art during this era.

Beyond just art, humanism also wanted people to take responsibility for their actions and morals outside of religion. It promoted a person's autonomous contribution to society in a way that put people and society first and religion second. Humanism emphasized the need for education to become a priority in order for people to learn how to be a good person before they learn how to be a good follower of religion.

This was a relatively drastic shift—no wonder it took up to three centuries! The mindset had suddenly shifted from mostly just honoring God and trying to survive to enjoying what it means to be human and educating oneself. Furthermore, people slowly began seeing each other as more valuable. If beforehand other people were simply followers of God, now they were more likely to be seen as equally important creations by God, and warranted more respect. People focused more on individuality and were allowed some degree of uniqueness finally. It is difficult to say definitively, but due to the Renaissance Era being regarded as the transition from darkness into a lighter time, it makes sense to assume that this era brought a more optimistic point of view.

Age of Enlightenment

In the 17th century, there came a new philosophical and intellectual movement—the Enlightenment. Here, the focus became rationality. The whirlwind of art, music, and philosophical literature was replaced by scientific discoveries and bold new ideas. Suddenly, people were focused on finding explanations for things outside of religion and art. Rather than thinking about what it means to be human-like in the previous era—people wanted answers to questions such as: Does the universe work without the influence of God? How do we rationally explain certain phenomena? What if we organized society with human well-being at the center and not religious ruling?

It was a tumultuous time and, most likely, not a much happier one than the Renaissance Era. However, these turbulent changes played a critical role in the development of society through the coming centuries, indicating a very strong shift in society's approach to life. People were finally waking up and getting the courage to fight back against the regimes that had been imposed on them. This era marks one of the most powerful examples of people breaking free from standards they were expected to simply accept. For example, writer Mary Wollstonecraft wrote *A Vindication of the Rights of Woman* in 1792, becoming an important icon in early feminism she sprouted from the changes exhibited throughout this era. Many people started thinking outside the box, questioning established routines, and encouraging people to think for themselves.

Can you identify the influence that the Age of Enlightenment has had on the modern world? Without these trailblazers, we would most likely have been far behind in societal progress. They paved the way for fighting for a better life and being proud of one's own beliefs. Although we still often face backlash from speaking our minds against societal standards, it is now much less of a taboo topic to discuss with others.

These changes are directly responsible for people's escape from lifestyles that didn't allow them to be happy and helped them stop being afraid to do so. Although negativity was probably *heightened* throughout this era due to people focusing on the bad so that they could fix it, it is a prime example of *good* negativity; negativity that lifts people up, rather than brings them down, which is a powerful mechanism for positive change.

Romanticism

The Romanticism Era is a direct product of the Enlightenment, but is considerably shorter than most of the previously examined eras, lasting roughly between 1800 and 1850. For this time period, society makes a return to celebrating life: art, music, literature, education, etcetera. But this time, we take it a step further. Rather than examining human life outside of religion, the focus was now on individualism itself. The forward-thinking fighters of the Enlightenment Era are the ones to thank for this.

Whereas the Age of Enlightenment centered around rationality and materials, Romanticism preferred the more subjective aspects of life. Individualism in the period of Romanticism allowed people to examine their emotions. The dust had slightly settled on fighting for freedom, and now, people were fighting for immaterial values.

People were finally allowed to feel and express their emotions with less opposition. They explored their beliefs deeper and were slightly more free to find ones that suited them better. They created art that reflected their passion and thought imagination was the best source of creation.

Aspects of Romanticism can quite clearly be seen today, with the recent increase in concern regarding mental health and emotional wellbeing reflecting this. It's not difficult, nowadays, to run into a person who proudly expresses their emotions through art, and that's truly a great thing to see. This period of Romanticism brought forth an important philosophy that continues to be relevant today: Don't ignore the more complicated and abstract parts of being human—express them.

Key Points

Let's look over the most important takeaways from Chapter 2:

- Understanding different approaches to life across time periods should inspire us to take our power back and not rely on the world to control our perceptions
- Society fluctuates between different perceptions of life
- Negativity is treated very differently across various cultures
- Changes in politics, the economy, and social security strongly influence our relationship with ourselves and our negative perception
- Trends exhibited in the past are key to our journey to positivity today

Chapter 3
Types of Negative Thinking

"Most misunderstandings in the world could be avoided if people would simply take the time to ask, 'What else could this mean?'"

— Shannon L. Alder

There's one reason why stopping negative thoughts tends to be so difficult: There are so many of them. Not only that, but even the term "negative thinking" is so broad, it encapsulates many different types. Negativity does not have only one form. Tackling all of them is what makes this task so challenging for many people.

Why Does Everything Seem So Bad?

You are obviously aware of the fact that your mind's negativity may be badly influencing your life, but are there perhaps some forms of negative thinking that you engage in without even realizing it? In this chapter, we'll be looking into what scientists call "cognitive distortions," which are essentially ways in which people perceive what happens around them in a distorted and negative manner. Such thoughts usually occur as incorrect assumptions, unrealistic self-criticisms, or even the denial of reality; and yet, their effects on you can often go unnoticed. When those thoughts start forming patterns, they become cognitive distortions—a term used to describe a person's inaccurate perception of reality. These cognitive distortions may then cause a person to believe false things about themselves or their place in the world, leading to various mental health issues.

Learning to recognize those cognitive distortions can help you avoid them and prevent them from leading to bad outcomes. Typical cognitive distortions include believing you are unworthy of success, thinking everyone sees you as lazy or incompetent or blaming yourself for the end of a relationship.

Examples of Negative Thinking

Catastrophizing

As the name indicates, catastrophizing occurs when we blow an issue out of proportion, making us react with a disproportionate level of emotion. This can often happen when we are already experiencing difficult emotions prior to the issue occurring. Being in a bad mood already makes us predisposed to seeing other things as worse than they are. However, catastrophizing can also originate from the issue itself, no matter how small it may be in reality. For many people, it may be because they have that reaction as a default setting—bad things seem *very* bad, and good things receive an underwhelming reaction. Let me give you an example: My mother was truly a light in my life, but the older I got, the more flaws I saw in her mentality at times; she was a worrier. She worried about me, she worried about my dad, she worried about her clients, and so on. When something bad would occur—as small as me having to delay my visit to her by a few days—it would be enough to ruin her mood for a week. On the other hand, her reaction to good surprises didn't meet the same fate—her happiness didn't last nearly as long.

I loved my mother with all my heart, and when I became old enough for her to fully trust me, she let me help her. I offered suggestions on how she can experience happiness more fully and sadness less invasively, and eventually we saw some progress. To make her feel less alone, I often participated in the exercises. When something bad would happen to us, we would answer the following questions together:

- What is my initial go-to reaction to this issue?
- Was this issue truly preventable by me or not?
- Will this issue affect me badly in one week, one month, or one year from now?
- Is there anything I can do going forward to make myself feel better?
- What have I learned from this issue, if anything?

With enough repetition, my mother's initial reaction of catastrophizing was slowly replaced by answering these questions. Suddenly, analyzing the issue through this lens was her new, go-to reaction.

Overgeneralization

Let's say you're a teacher. It's the end of the semester and the students submit their feedback on your performance. One student said you failed to explain things clearly enough, so they ended the semester more confused than they had started it. Instead of accepting the feedback and vowing to be clearer going forward, you take it to heart, and start thinking, "I'm a terrible teacher." Even if feedback from the rest of the class was positive, you still fixate on that one comment and apply it to your entire performance, to your whole career—you are a terrible teacher and that's that.

Not too helpful, is it? This is how overgeneralization operates—it makes us fixate on one singular detail, overlooking the abundance of others. This one tiny thing is given far too much importance and can become the entire way we view ourselves. Rather than acknowledging that we all have strengths and weaknesses, we analyze ourselves only through the context of that one pesky, disappointing detail.

You may ask, then: What is the difference between catastrophizing and overgeneralizing? Both of them take small things and blow them out of proportion, right? The difference is that catastrophizing is a mental or emotional overreaction to a certain incident, but it doesn't define your perspective of someone or something. Overgeneralizing is more potent as a cognitive distortion because it warps your entire sense of who you are, or of what another person or situation is, based on one isolated incident.

Emotional reasoning
<u></u>

This may be one of the clearest examples of cognitive distortion, and it is directly linked to our emotions. A common reason some people claim they hate love is that it makes you act stupid. In a way, it makes perfect sense what they mean; emotional reasoning is to blame here.

If a person has a romantic partner whom they are either infatuated or in love with, their judgment will likely be clouded. If this partner is not treating them properly, they are far more likely to excuse it due to their feelings—unlike their friends who probably want them to break it off. Their intense emotions and appreciation for this person make it hard to be truly objective about their actions.

The way this can become a cognitive distortion is through their reality becoming warped: Their partner may be bad for them, but they continue to stay with them, thinking it's worth it. When our emotions overpower our logic, it isn't always meaningful or romantic—sometimes, it can be damaging. The older we get, the better we tend to navigate these waters, but a good thing to do is to have an objective support system around you that can signal if you're ever succumbing to this emotional rationalization.

Fortune-telling

Not to be the bearer of bad news, but this one isn't as sweet as it sounds. We all wish we could sometimes definitively know the outcome of something without having to risk it first, but the fortune-telling we're talking about here doesn't let you do that.

I honestly believe that would be quite counterproductive. Knowing how our lives will turn out takes the accountability out of them, and therefore, the exploration. With this knowledge, we would stop trying altogether and simply let life happen *to* us, not *for* us.

Even if we aren't able to predict the future, some people's minds still attempt to—and, spoiler alert—they're not very good at it.

Fortune-telling in the form of negative thinking is what I lightly touched on in Chapter 1: We're not certain of what will happen, so we assume an undesirable outcome out of emotional protection. Does it emotionally protect us, though? Is thinking that we are bound to fail without even trying truly beneficial? Obviously, no.

Fortune-telling in a cycle of negativity only makes us do it again and again. To break out of it, we need to actively go against its nature. If your mind manages to convince you that you won't get that job—apply anyway! The only way to reprogram your mind is through conscious repetition. Just like my mother answering those anti-catastrophizing questions, it will eventually become second nature. Take chances, take risks, and stop letting your fortune-telling instincts influence you.

Mind-reading

Much like fortune-telling, this one is a bit of a guessing game. The same reasons we fortune-tell are behind mind-reading as well: We are too afraid of the unknown.

Mind-reading in the context of cognitive distortions boils down to assuming we know exactly what other people think and feel, especially what they think and feel about *us*.

When you aren't entirely sure what someone thinks of you (so, most of the time), you might be tempted to find out. When we like someone romantically, for example, many of us would pay good money to find out how they feel about us. Instead, we often resort to dissecting every little thing that they say or do. When we are left stumped and desperate for answers, we may start to create our own theories. When these theories get coupled with the anxiety or paranoia of not knowing, they tend to come out quite negatively.

This tendency to mind-read often leads us to feel worse about certain relationships than is necessary. If we managed to convince ourselves that someone doesn't like us, we might analyze every one of their actions as passive-aggressive, for example. Since most of us are not truly clairvoyant, our mind-reading attempts can be quite detrimental to ourselves and our relationships with others.

Imperatives

One of my favorite songs of all time is Beverley Knight's "Shoulda Woulda Coulda," though it's the kind of song I take in without paying much attention to the words. When you listen to the lyrics, however, Beverley sings about a deteriorated relationship and how her "shoulda woulda couldas" (her reflections on how things could have gone down) indicate that she is out of time. I don't believe in this; there is always time, at least to try again, if nothing else.

This song happens to showcase an instance of imperatives in terms of cognitive distortion. Imperatives occur when we make ourselves feel bad for feeling bad. If you have horrible anxiety when it comes to public speaking, for example, imperative thinking would cause you to think that you shouldn't have this anxiety. This thought process makes you angrier, more defensive, and less likely to be able to fix the issue. Only through acceptance of your anxiety can you go about making adjustments.

Inability to be wrong

Let's all admit it—it feels selfishly good to be right! It's that annoying little feeling that might overpower all others. In extreme cases, the inability to be wrong becomes a cognitive distortion.

When this is pushed to the extreme, the inability to be wrong makes a person prioritize being right over their relationship with the person they're arguing against, as well as over logic and proof. When someone fails to accept their errors, they not only put themselves against an impossible standard, but they risk losing the ability to learn from others. If you never see yourself as being incorrect about anything in the first place, then there isn't much room for that growth to occur.

Jumping to conclusions

This is a kind of distorted thinking that goes hand in hand with the inability to be proven wrong, fortune-telling, and mind-reading. Some of us are more guilty of this than others, and it's sometimes due to anxiety. If we have an anxious attachment style, for example, we may have the tendency to assume the worst of our partners. Imagine they had gone out to dinner with friends and hadn't texted you in three hours. Do you assume their phone is dead? Or maybe, they lost it? Or do you assume they got intoxicated and are now cheating on you?

Even without knowing the real answer, you may be so distraught at the thought of them betraying you that your whole night is ruined. The reality may be completely different than what we push ourselves to assume—jumping to conclusions is helping no one.

Labeling

We are constantly attributing labels to people, places, things, situations, and even ourselves. If we believe a certain family function is going to be awkward, then we don't attend; if we perceive someone at work to be 'fake,' we try to stay away from them; if we think of ourselves as a bad friend, we are more likely to act like one.

People with mental health problems or even self-esteem issues tend to put the most negative labels on themselves, and we all know how we can be our own harshest critics. If someone sees themselves as dumb, unattractive, or bad at their job, they eventually grow into that mold because their negative perception strips them of the will to work around those self-inflicted labels.

These labels focus on one aspect of a situation and discredit the others. By labeling, we are effectively throwing away potential and giving up on improvement.

Mental filtering

Just like a strainer, our minds will sometimes only remember certain parts of our past, whether it is consciously or not. Mental filtering is when a person only remembers the negative aspects of something. Perhaps you hated your time in high school, but why? Is it truly because everything was awful or do you simply happen to remember the worst of it?

We often say we hated a time in our lives because of something in particular that we didn't enjoy back then. However, by doing this, we diminish everything that we *did* enjoy. Maybe your last job was boring you out of your mind, but what if you really liked your coworkers? Does that period still hold an awful place in your past or could you acknowledge both the good and bad?

Minimizing

I think of minimizing as a present version of mental filtering: Rather than see the world for what it is (good and bad), a person focuses mostly on the bad. By minimizing our good experiences—no matter how small they are—we prevent our own experience of happiness. For example, when you chalk up your accomplishments to mere luck, disregarding the work you had to put into them, or when you acknowledge said work but tell yourself it was very easy to do, the victory doesn't count.

To stop minimizing, we need to actively fight against it. When you get the urge to think that something discredits your experience, try reframing your thinking to a more accurate representation of it.

Personalization

Personalization, or self-blame, happens when you take problems or details that have nothing to do with you and make them all about you. The textbook example is, of course, a child blaming themselves for their parent's divorce. Terrible, isn't it? As if we didn't already struggle enough with the things that directly pertain to us, we also carry the burden of guilt over things we have no control over. But that's exactly how overthinking and negative thinking in general work: They create a vicious cycle that's hard to break out of, spreading to include the things that should be peripheral to them.

Polarization

We've sort of been conditioned to see things in clear-cut spectrums; black or white, good or bad, yes or no, and so on. This is what we call polarization, or dichotomous thinking. This all-or-nothing state of mind makes it hard to approach issues with any nuance or room for compromise. But issues are complex, and shouldn't be boxed into one simple category.

In some cases, this can manifest as extreme indecisiveness. If you have two options to choose from and you are someone who polarizes their issues, you may be convinced that one of the options is right while the other is wrong. The pressure of wanting to choose the 'right' one is what makes it so difficult. In reality, however, both choices are probably fine but lead to different outcomes.

Another common example has to do with competitiveness. In this case, the person would be completely dissatisfied unless they felt like they were the best at something. This 'all-or-nothing' makes people feel inadequate and dissatisfied with something that they could still have considered an accomplishment.

Control fallacies

There are two ways in which control fallacies can manifest: The first comes when you feel desperate because you have no control over anything in your life and are therefore powerless to stop it; the second happens when you conclude that you have absolute control, and are therefore entirely to blame for any faux-pas.

Many people I know who suffer from control fallacies often oscillate between the two, and that's no way to live life. The ones that managed to escape this torturous mindset did so by consciously going against these trends. When they told me about how their life seemed to be spinning out of control, we worked together to find things that they felt like they *could* control. When the opposite happened and they were blaming themselves for every little thing going wrong, I helped them be at peace with letting go. Suffering through control fallacies can feel extremely isolating. Talking these feelings through with a trusted person may make you realize things aren't as dire as they seem.

Fairness fallacies

Life isn't fair, right? We've all heard this or said it ourselves a million times. But analyzing situations in terms of how just or unjust they are, not only falls under the dichotomous spectrum we've already discussed, but it also tends to be less than helpful in the context of mental health. This is especially true when we consider that fairness is not an objective thing, and will therefore change according to the person— what is fair to you might not be fair to the next person.

If someone in your life seems to be progressing faster than you are, your sense of envy might make you believe it's only their luck. Furthermore, why don't *you* have the same luck? It must be just an unfair distribution of luck, right? By believing this, you blame abstract factors rather than taking responsibility for your own experience.

Let's say your coworker got a promotion you were trying to get—do you think this is unfair? If you do, you are more likely to stay focused on this one failure rather than thinking of ways to improve your future.

Change fallacies

Believing that someone or something will eventually change to suit your needs is a fallacy of change. When I had my first serious boyfriend at 19, I constantly believed things would get better between us if he just grew up a bit more. It boiled down to me projecting my own needs and desires onto him and then getting disappointed when I didn't see the results I expected. He was certainly no angel, but I do take responsibility for the fact that I hadn't ended it sooner—I *chose* to stay and wait for him to make the changes; I could have reacted accordingly and cut him loose the moment I picked up on that, but I kept hoping he would change. More often than not, if someone is not willing to meet your needs, the only thing that needs to be changed is your approach.

Untangling Cognitive Distortions

Now, not every pattern of negative thinking will fit neatly into one of the definitions listed in this chapter, and they can even overlap. You probably related to most of these examples, remembering one time or another where you were guilty of them; I relate to some of them more than others. What usually happens is that one case of negative thinking leads directly to another, then another, creating a complex chain that is hard to break. Thankfully, by doing the necessary work, you can get there. It all starts with recognizing if any of these negative thinking types are recurring in your everyday life, on the brink of forming a habit, if you don't already have one. Once you've identified problem areas, there are ways to fight back.

Key Points

Let's look over the most important takeaways from Chapter 3:

- There are 16 types of common negative thinking
- It's important to understand and assess our symptoms of negative thinking in order for us to make the necessary changes
- We often get so used to these types of negative thinking to the point where we don't realize that we are not being objective
- Admitting our negative thinking tendencies is the first step toward improving our positivity

Chapter 4
Negative Thoughts: How and Why They Occur

"What we think determines what happens to us, so if we want to change our lives, we need to stretch our minds."

— Wayne W. Dyer

I'm sure I'm not the first to tell you that the brain remains a major mystery of ours, and the parts of it that we do understand are very complex. If you aren't the most technical person (such as myself), you won't want to learn every intricate detail of negative thinking on a neurological level. I am a strong believer, though, that knowing some basics of how our brains function allows our experiences to not only be validated but seem less abstract. Negative thinking has very real, biological explanations that help us understand why it occurs and how we can deal with it.

Stressing About Stressing

Constant stress is bad for you—we're all aware of this, but do most of us even know why? Beyond just the unpleasant feeling of being under constant pressure, the issue lies deeper.

The amygdala in our brains is a small, almond-shaped part of our brain that is largely responsible for emotional management, as well as processing threatening stimulants. However, its respective size and the strength of its connections with the other regions within the brain determine how strongly a person reacts to such stimuli. For example, a study at the Stanford University School of Medicine found that the larger a child's amygdala and the stronger its connections were, the more anxiety they experienced in everyday life (Bergeron, 2013).

What, you may ask, causes the increase in size of the amygdala? Several things, unfortunately, including anxiety and depression; but, among that list is a factor common to most of the population: stress. Chronic and heavy stress not only shrinks the prefrontal cortex of the brain (which could affect a person's social behavior), but it simultaneously enlarges the amygdala. This, in turn, makes a person's brain far too receptive to stress, meaning they can become overwhelmed from much less.

Cortisol

To put it simply, our stress causes the production of cortisol. Whenever we are stressed or under pressure, our brain triggers the production of this specific hormone that influences us in several ways. Cortisol is produced and released in the adrenal glands, which are little, triangle-shaped parts located atop each of our kidneys; these are our body's main stress hormones—our built-in alarm system. If danger strikes, cortisol kicks in and we are locked into fight-or-flight mode.

You might be thinking "A-ha! So cortisol is to blame for me being so anxious all the time." The truth is, cortisol is an integral part of being human and has helped our species to survive for as long as we have. Not only has it been helpful in life-threatening situations where time was of the essence, but it is also responsible for:

- Regulating your blood pressure
- Controlling your sleep cycle
- Keeping various inflammation down
- Increasing your blood sugar
- Managing the carbohydrates, fats, and proteins you consume
- Boosting your energy levels

With a list of such benefits, it's hard to believe that something so helpful can also be quite damaging. Let's put it this way: Imagine cortisol is an employee and your body is the company it works for. That employee is a valued member of the company, providing great work within reason and delivering great results. But the moment that employee is overworked and pushed around by the company, their productivity is hindered and they can no longer provide the ideal results, through no fault of their own. In the case of cortisol, then, if your body keeps perceiving danger and setting it in motion, the hormone's production will be sent into overdrive. Before long, the little tasks that cortisol performs, which were listed above, are thrown out of whack and start being threats themselves.

Your needs differ at different times; this is especially relevant in the case of perceived danger. If your body is on high alert, for example, cortisol can alter or shut down functions that get in its way, such as your digestive, reproductive, and immune systems. After the danger or pressure has subsided, your cortisol levels should calm down, meaning your bodily functions should be brought back to normal. If you're under constant stress, however, the alarm button stays on, causing your body's most important functions to potentially derail, leading to several health problems, including:

- Chronic headaches
- Heart disease
- Memory and concentration problems
- Digestion issues
- Trouble sleeping
- Weight gain
- Anxiety, depression, and other mental health issues

Now, do keep in mind that there are certain medical conditions that can produce too much cortisol, such as having a nodule or mass in your adrenal gland, or a tumor in your brain's pituitary gland. Too much cortisol can cause the condition known as Cushing's syndrome, leading to rapid weight gain, easily-bruised skin, muscle weakness, diabetes, and other health problems. Cortisol in low volumes, on the other hand, can lead to Addison's disease, which results in fatigue, diarrhea, and other issues.

Under normal circumstances, however, what keeps people under stress (therefore, producing more cortisol) is their own perception of the world. If their brains are wired to perceive everything unknown as a danger, then the body responds accordingly by creating more and more cortisol, possibly causing the whole system to go haywire.

The big takeaway here is that negative thinking is a much-needed reaction for our bodies due to the benefits of cortisol. This is exactly why I take so much issue with people wanting to eradicate negative thinking; that is not only unnatural and impossible, it's simply illogical. We need our negative impulses to navigate this rocky world around us, otherwise we *would* fall victim to its dangers. Issues only arise when we start seeing danger when there is probably none—we become a danger to ourselves. We need to reframe those negative thoughts and adapt to them, not get rid of them.

Brain Fog

Chronic stress is also a very common cause of brain fog—a state in which a person feels particularly forgetful, unconcentrated, and has a lack of clarity. Brain fog is often coupled with feeling physically tired, but not always; it has many different potential causes, ranging from pregnancy to various physical illnesses.

Another cause of brain fog happens to be the high production of the previously mentioned hormone of cortisol. Too much of this stress hormone tends to overwhelm the brain, exhausting it to the point of its inability to properly function. This affects nearly every region of the brain in a similar way to how chronic lack of sleep does—all of our mental functions start to suffer.

Brain fog can last continuously for several months if your brain is extremely overwhelmed or if no adjustments are occurring. If a person is not aware of what brain fog is or places a rigid amount of pressure on themselves, they might not even know they are experiencing it or will force themselves to simply push past it. Unfortunately, both lead to negative outcomes that only worsen the symptoms. They might start forgetting more and more deadlines, making errors in their work even with proofreading, and having their overall productivity and well-being suffer.

The only truly effective solution to brain fog is to stop doing what you're doing. What I mean by this is that your life requires a complete overhaul if your brain fog has been consistently getting worse or has lasted for more than a week. In this scenario, de-stressing isn't just an option, it's imperative.

Mental Health Complications

Negative thinking has many potential sources. We've gone over how time period trends, societal standards, and cultural differences can influence us to think one way or another. There are more reasons, however, that take control away from us.

No one asks to be mentally ill or go through traumatic experiences, yet they continue to happen to people. They might blame genetics, family members, or simply chance, depending on what caused them to have this fate. Understanding what other factors might influence your negative thinking can help you find the appropriate route to recovery.

Chronic negative thinking is a common result and symptom of PTSD, or Post-Traumatic Stress Disorder. PTSD is a mental health issue that follows a traumatic or particularly distressing event. A lot of people associate this illness with something like military combat, but in reality, PTSD can arise from an array of different experiences.

Even without PTSD, a person's rough history can influence their mental health to become significantly more negative. Experiencing emotional abuse growing up or having emotionally absent guardians can cause the child's brain to develop in a way that makes them more susceptible to depression, anxiety, attachment issues, and consequently, negative thinking.

Importance of Sleep

It is considerably easier to treat problems and fix issues when we can *see* them—at least, in a way that makes it undeniably clear that they are indeed real. With issues that have effects on our mental well-being, many of us struggle to understand what has to be done.

When someone breaks their arm, the protocol is clear: get to a hospital, get a cast put on, wait six or so weeks for it to somewhat heal, and take off the cast. You don't wait six months before going to the hospital, hoping it heals on its own, and you certainly don't go back to using your broken arm after putting a mere band aid on it. So, why do we do this so often to our mental issues?

The science is quite clear on the fact that our physical health influences the health of our brains, their functioning, and their mental well-being. Even if we do not physically see a concrete connection between the two, it is unquestionably there.

Sleep Is for the Strong

The effects of chronic lack of sleep on your mind include:

- **Lower alertness and concentration.** Sleep is a critical time for the brain. It's vital for the brain's plasticity, memory consolidation, and simply giving it a rest from conscious thought and focus. Without this rest, the brain cannot hold attention for nearly as long as it could otherwise and can't react as adequately to stimuli. The brain is like a muscle—if you keep working it out without any rest, it will eventually fail to pick up the dumbbell.

- **Worsened memory.** The REM (Rapid Eye Movement) cycle of sleep is a time for the brain to build and strengthen the memories it has created throughout the day. If this stage of sleep is not reached or is of poor quality or short length, the brain fails to adequately do so. Not only does it retain much less information, but in some cases, it can even create *false* memories.

- **Lack of cognitive flexibility.** If the brain is exhausted, running on extra time, it cannot possibly adapt to an array of new things. With proper sleep and good cognitive flexibility, a person's brain can easily adapt to a new environment or situation. However, without those factors, the brain is incapable of handling such new information and figuring out how to act accordingly. This makes meeting new people, starting a new job, and even hearing surprising news difficult to handle.

- **Worse emotional processing.** With a lack of sleep, your brain's efficiency is suffering. This is true even on a one-time basis; if you were to pull an all-nighter just once, the following day you are instantly more likely to be in a bad mood, react strongly to minor inconveniences, and manage your emotions poorly. If this occurs even from one night, imagine how it would look on a near-daily basis. Basically, negative thinking skyrockets as a result of poor sleep.

- **Poor decision-making.** Ever feel indecisive due to negativity? Well, this is multiplied if you're a victim of a rough sleep schedule. Without the proper seven to nine hours of sleep, your brain is running on overdrive, not knowing which way is up. With your brain being less capable of fully grasping the stimuli it's being presented with, it has a harder time understanding what the best response would be. If you're forced to make tough decisions, not only will this seem even more stressful than usual, it will feel riskier, as well.

There are several recommendations to get your sleep schedule on track. We've all heard them, but only a few of us actually follow through. I'll present a few tips that helped me straighten out my sleep schedule after a few years at an extremely demanding job, which are now simply part of my habitual routine:

- **Have a bedtime!** I used to be the type of
  person to go to bed when I felt really tired and not
  a minute earlier. There's a reason I did this, which
  is common to many of us: revenge bedtime
  procrastination—the act of going to bed later in
  favor of doing things you didn't get to do
  throughout the day. Oftentimes, the tasks that we
  end up doing instead of sleeping are hobbies or
  methods of relaxation that we simply do not have
  time for during the daytime. If you finish work
  late, you might be eager to get an episode of your
  favorite show in before you go to sleep. The victim
  in this scenario still ends up being yourself—or
  rather, future-you waking up the following
  morning. Another thing to look out for is
  something called the "second wind." This is a term
  used to describe a sudden increase in energy levels
  after you had been feeling tired in the evening.
  This second wind often fools people into thinking
  they shouldn't go to bed when really it is the
  body's last resort to try and help you do the things
  you're staying up for. Once I realized that it was
  merely my second wind giving me the ability to
  stay up until 1:30 am, I started listening to my
  body for the first time.
- **Kill the blue light.** Ah, yet another flaw of
  technological progress—the blue light. The blue
  light wavelengths emitted by various technological
  devices, such as your phone, laptop, and TV are all
  damaging your body's natural circadian rhythm.
  Now, we might not be able to avoid it completely,
  but there are ways that you can lessen the harm it
  causes you. Buying blue light glasses is one great

way, but the best I can recommend is to simply put away your devices at least one hour to half an hour before bed. If this goes against your habits, it might be tough to kick, so try finding an equally-engaging replacement; this could include an adult coloring book, doing some light bedtime yoga or stretching, reading a pleasant book, or going for a calming walk. I'm someone who gets bored easily, so I tend to rotate between these options; I was shocked at how nice it was to look at something other than my phone screen right before bed.

- **Treat your wind-down routine as non-negotiable.** Arianna Huffington— businesswoman and founder of *The Huffington Post*—is a very prominent advocate for the importance of sleep. She says that "a set ritual helps tell your mind and body that it's time to begin to wind down. My own involves turning off all my electronic devices [...] Then, I take a hot bath [...] Sometimes I'll have a cup of chamomile or lavender tea" (Kondo, n.d). If someone as busy and impressively successful as Arianna Huffington can make a relaxing wind-down routine a priority, it should inspire others to do so as well. She has a great point: Our bodies get used to habits and start to recognize triggers. If you incorporate a relaxing routine at nighttime, eventually you will not only crave it, but you will likely fall asleep easier.

Key Points

Let's look over the most important takeaways from Chapter 4:

- The effects of negative thinking go beyond just a bad mood
- Continuous negative thinking can cause some physical symptoms and make life even harder to live
- Aspects such as sleep and physical health should not be overlooked when trying to improve our negative thinking—they play a very large role
- Over-productivity and lack of rest ultimately lead to worse productivity

Chapter 5
A Skewed Perception

"Chains of habit are too light to be felt until they are too heavy to be broken."

— Warren Buffet

As rational as we may think we are, people are extremely biased—we often fail to be objective. Like many other psychological phenomena, this may come from both environmental and innate factors.

Briefly mentioned in Chapter 1 was impact bias—the phenomenon responsible for us overestimating our potential happiness and potential sadness. According to a study by Timothy Wilson and Daniel Gilbert (2005), one of the biggest contributors to our impact bias is focalism. Focalism is kind of like tunnel vision; when we imagine something awful happening to us, such as a painful breakup for example, focalism causes us to focus solely on this event. Realistically, if you were to break up with your romantic partner, that would not be the only thing happening in your life. At first, it may feel like it is, but quite soon the realization will start to set in that you have dozens of other things going for you. Focalism, however, makes us forget the influence of those other events in our life, even throughout a drastic event.

Another thing to remember is that people are constantly bored. We are built to be constantly craving something more, something new. How is this relevant to impact bias? Well, if impact bias causes us to expect ourselves to become considerably happier once we finally get that promotion we've wanted, it will not be enough. Why? Because we will get bored.

Boredom facilitates change (or, at least, it should). People are meant to get so used to their circumstances that they get bored and start to think innovatively to improve them. Therefore, when you finally get that long-awaited promotion, you *will* be happy, but not for nearly as long as you may have thought. Instead, you will get accustomed to this new life of yours and will soon enough have your eye set on something even bigger. Now, the same is applied to unpleasant future situations as well. You may be completely heartbroken for a few weeks, months, or even a year following your breakup, but you *will* eventually get bored of that as well. You are made to get used to your circumstances —good or bad. No feeling will remain constant throughout your life; you will likely want new things, no matter how many you get.

Negativity Bias

It's a known fact that we tend to dwell on the negatives much more than we do on the positives. Of course, the severity of this varies from person to person, but most people need to make an active effort to balance out what they focus on. Choosing to dwell on the positives requires a conscious decision for change.

Criticism has a greater impact than praise, just as bad news draws more attention than good news—it's no wonder you see nothing but tragedy every time you turn on your TV. You'll rarely see headlines about major positive changes around the world, but something negative will loom on almost every page of the newspaper. Partly, this is because paying attention to something negative can literally save someone's life, whereas noticing something positive simply boosts our moods. Another reason for this is that negative events have a greater impact on our brains, which some psychologists refer to as "the negative bias" (or negativity bias). This bias can have a powerful effect on your decisions, behavior, and even your relationships.

The negativity bias is your tendency to not only register negative stimuli more easily but also to overwhelmingly dwell on those triggering events. It's a psychological phenomenon that explains, for example, why bad first impressions are so difficult to overcome, or why traumas of the past tend to have such long, lingering effects. In pretty much every interaction we have, we are more likely to both notice and remember the person's negative aspects far more than the positive ones. You could be having the best day ever, receive some disappointing news, and have that be enough to ruin your otherwise perfect day. Essentially, your bias makes you pay much more attention to the bad things, giving them far more significance than they have. Negativity bias effectively causes us to turn over our emotional control to unpleasant events.

The negativity bias starts to emerge in infancy. Babies tend to pay greater attention to positive facial expressions and tones of voice, but this all changes when they reach one year of age. Around this stage, and sometimes earlier, babies begin to experience greater brain responses to negative stimuli. This further tips us off that the negativity bias is indeed more innate than it is cultivated through our worldly experiences.

Neuroscientific evidence shows us that there is a greater process of response in the brain to negative stimuli, even in adulthood. Psychologist John Cacioppo performed a test by showing participants several pictures of either positive, negative, or neutral scenarios; he then observed the electrical activity in the participants' brains and found that the negative images produced a much stronger response in the cerebral cortex than either of the other two categories of pictures (MIUC, 2017). Several factors have been identified so far as being responsible for our negativity bias.

Motivation
—————

Research suggests that the negativity bias influences one's motivation to complete any task. Much like how some people thrive under pressure, we tend to have less motivation when there is something to be gained from our work than when there is something to be lost. Silly, isn't it? This means that if your boss promises you a bonus for meeting a certain quota, you'll be less motivated to meet it than you would be if you were threatened with being fired instead. The reason for this is that we are so wired to focus on the negatives that even if you are promised something good, like that bonus, you will still be more focused on what you might lose in the meantime (for example, hours of rest). If you were instead threatened with being let go, then you already know what you stand to lose. This is not a push for toxic work environments or draconian methods of leadership, but rather an explanation of how powerful our fear is.

Bad news

If you diligently check the news on the daily, you are likely to meet with tragedy after tragedy. This is because media outlets picked up on the negativity bias a long time ago and choose to exploit it for views and popularity. Pain, gruesomeness, and disaster have a shock factor—or wow factor—that allows that type of news to gain a lot of traction, quickly. The negativity bias also causes us to believe bad news over good news, much like how we believe an insult to be true much more easily than a compliment.

With this constant influx of negativity from the news, we are further programmed to receive it more easily. This, in turn, causes us to be more susceptible to it from other sources as well, and even expect the worst for our future selves.

Politics

In a world as politically unstable as the one we currently live in, generalizations are often hard to make. People that make up a certain political party may often be lumped into a stereotype by opposing parties, but in reality, tend to have some differing beliefs. Regardless, statistics offer us a perspective of trends that we may choose to deduce information from or not.

So far, psychologists have found that conservatives tend to have stronger responses to negative information than liberals do (Gjersoe, 2017). People who consider themselves politically conservative are more likely to rate ambiguous stimuli as threatening, causing opposing party members to view them as rather defensive in regard to hot-button topics. These differences might explain why some people are more likely to value things such as tradition and safety, while others are more in favor of rapid change and progress.

Suffering the Consequences

All of the listed factors above can help us understand the source of our negativity bias and why it is so potent in our lives. The following section will focus on the *outcomes* of negativity bias and why it can be quite harmful.

Relationships

The negativity bias can have a profound effect on your relationships; particularly, it can lead to you expecting the worst from others, even without having any real supporting evidence for this assumption. You might expect your parents to react badly to a decision you've made, such as a career change. If your defense system is already on high alert, chances are that the moment one of your parents says something as innocuous as, "are you sure?", you may perceive it as confirmation of your negative suspicions. Overall, our negativity bias makes us eager to confirm our negative expectations.

Where relationships are concerned, it's important to remember that negative comments carry more weight than positive ones; and since everyone is predisposed to a negativity bias, being aware of your tendency to fixate on the negative, you can start finding ways to let others off the hook a bit more.

Decision-making

Nobel Prize-winning researchers and friends, Kahneman and Tversky, once found that when making decisions, people often place greater weight on negative aspects than they do on positive ones (Lewis, 2016). This tendency is bound to have an impact on the choices people make and the risks they are willing to take. Going back to the career change example, maybe you want to switch lanes for all the best reasons: your current job isn't fulfilling enough, it doesn't pay as well as you'd like, and the people you work with are a bit toxic. Just as you start tossing the idea around of finding a new job, you start worrying about what might happen if you quit—that you won't make any income, that the employment gap might look bad on your resumé, or that you could wind up at another job that's just as bad, if not worse—and you ultimately decide against it.

Most of us go through life afraid of taking truly big chances because we believe we wouldn't be able to bear it if the results weren't positive. Big rewards come with big risks, no matter how inconvenient that may be. If we don't take the risk, then there are simply no results to reap of any kind, be they positive or negative. Assuming the worst possible outcome does not protect you from the bad, it only prevents you from getting the good.

People perception

To our caveman mind, the unknown equals danger. For this same reason, bad first impressions are *really* hard to shake off. When we do not know someone, we will make our conclusion based on the little information that we are provided with. If during our first meeting they happen to be 15 minutes late, that is all that we have to go off of, making us instantly perceive them as unpunctual and even perhaps disrespectful. The same approach can apply to settings and situations; if you have a bad experience somewhere the first time around, it's very likely you won't want to return to that place again.

Pining for Victimhood?

There is another possible psychological explanation for negativity bias. Except, not many people ever consider it and even fewer people will admit to it. The phenomenon I'm talking about is something I like to call "the weaponization of victimhood."

The term "underdog" is coined to represent someone who is perceived as less likely to succeed against their competition. Except, even the word itself has now gained certain respectability; people often tend to root for the underdog, not in spite of their proneness to failure, but *because* of it. This has rightfully given a certain power to people in positions of lesser authority than others. They are effectively uplifted by others' support to see them succeed against all odds.

In many societal issues, this is a fantastic thing to see—people who are the victims of injustices or mistreatment being supported and rooted for by others. However, this phenomenon can inspire some people to seek support *through* victimhood.

For example, a person may always blame their circumstances, other people, or pure chance, for all their misfortunes. Now, we have all had wrenches thrown into our lives seemingly out of the blue; however, if someone fails to take accountability for absolutely every mishap in their life, they are likely seeking pity for validation. They might want their life to seem harder and more unfair than everyone else's so that their shortcomings are not blamed on them.

This mechanism of pining for victimhood not only takes away from the severity of real victims of injustice but makes negativity the default outlook of the individual themselves.

Snap Out of It!

If you feel the negative thoughts creeping in and you want to push yourself out of that situation, then the best thing to do is to immediately dive into something else altogether—something that you love doing and that is sure to keep your mind busy with positivity. Our mood greatly influences the way we think, as well as the other way around, so if you choose to do something satisfying, your mood will be uplifted and your thoughts will follow suit. If you start over-thinking or spiraling into negativity at work, for example, then your options are not as broad as they otherwise would be. However, even doing something mundane can help take your mind off of negative thoughts, as long as you aim your focus at something else. So, at work, simply try giving it your all; boring or not, thoughts only have power if you give them attention. If you have a void in your positivity, fill it with accomplishments!

Establishing New Patterns

It's important to keep in mind that the solutions mentioned above might be quick fixes, but not long-lasting, let alone permanent ones. The entire premise of this book is to decrease excess negativity by turning it into something positive; but, before I get to explaining how to do so, we need to establish how one should go about *managing* their negativity.

Stop negative self-talk

If you start paying attention to the type of thoughts that run through your mind, you will probably be able to pick up on specific patterns. If you perhaps tend to think "I shouldn't have said what I said, I bet I offended them," pretty often, it may be indicating an underlying issue. This type of thought can mean any number of things: Maybe you need to start being mindful of people's feelings *before* you say something; or, perhaps you have some form of social anxiety that leads you to pick away at everything you say to others, even when no harm is done. Reframing your habitual negative thoughts includes assessing them: Are they telling you something about yourself?

Savor positive moments

Since it takes more effort for us to recognize and remember positive experiences, making sure that you give extra importance to them when they happen can help you see the world in a more balanced, less negatively-biased way. Even if all it is, is being extra mindful of your morning coffee, it's worth doing—little tweaks can lead to the biggest changes. You do it so often that it's easy to disregard how much you enjoy it, but if you were suddenly stripped of that simple pleasure, you would miss it like crazy. You could even try replaying positive moments in your head the same way you do to the negative ones and think about all the good feelings they gave you.

Key Points

Let's look over the most important takeaways from Chapter 5:

- The negativity bias is ingrained in our brains, often making us notice the bad far more than the good
- The negativity bias affects every area of our lives
- Not taking accountability for our failures hurts us in the long run—playing the victim every time prevents us from growing
- Breaking out of the cycle of the negativity bias requires a change in habits and consistency

Chapter 6
Practical Steps Towards a Happier Life

"Happiness depends upon ourselves."

— Aristotle

A simple quote, isn't it? It's one of my favorites, and yet its significance doesn't click for us until we internalize its meaning.

Since negative thinking is going to be a part of us whether we want it to be or not, we might as well turn it into something productive. In this chapter, we explore how to use negative thoughts to your benefit, directly proving that getting *rid* of negative thoughts is not the solution to obtaining happiness—only reframing them is.

Ancient philosophers like Marcus Aurelius, Seneca, and Epictetus often practiced an exercise called *premeditatio malorum*—the "premeditation of evils." This activity aimed to foresee the negative things that could happen in life, such as losing one's job and becoming homeless, for example. Those philosophers believed that by imagining the worst-case scenario in advance, they might overcome their fears of negative experiences and therefore prepare for them ahead of time. So, while most people around them were focused on reaping success, those philosophers thought about how they might manage failure. That way of thinking is known as inversion and it can be a great skill to master.

Inversion

Inversion puts the focus on errors and setbacks which may not be obvious at first glance. It makes you assess an outcome you wouldn't want in a way that allows you to think through it rationally, and it starts by you asking yourself how *not* to do something. After all, sometimes it is far more important to consider why people fail at anything rather than how they succeed; success can be hard to emulate, but it's important to know what you can and should avoid. For example, if you're trying to think of innovative ways to get a work project to the next level, you can start by listing the things that would get in the way of it being finished or promoted. By identifying the most likely flaws and barriers that you might succumb to, you can become aware of how to remove, avoid, or prevent them. In addition, you might even be able to get some great ideas on what should be done just by doing the opposite of what you now know you *shouldn't* do.

This method of thinking falls in line perfectly with the notion we're now accustomed to: that people take in negative stimuli more readily than they do positive stimuli. Furthermore, it doesn't shame you for this tendency of yours, but rather, encourages you to use it to your benefit. So, if you think, "how can I alienate a customer?", you will know what not to do and, by default, what you *can* do to attract said customers. On the other hand, if you were to sit down and think, "how can I attract customers?", you're bound to have a harder time brainstorming ideas. Below are a few practical examples of inversion thinking you can apply to your day-to-day life, courtesy of best-selling author James Clear (n.d).

Project Management

Clear defends an application of inversion thinking dubbed "failure premortem." It starts with you taking into account the most important project you're working on right now. It then asks you to fast-forward six months into the future and assume the project has failed; how did that happen? What did you do wrong? So, essentially, it is asking you to think of your most important goal and to ask yourself, "what could make this possibly go wrong?"

This strategy is also known as the "kill the company" exercise because it can be used to spell out how a company might fail based on any given project. The key goal is to identify any potential challenges so that you can develop a plan to prevent them ahead of time.

It must be pointed out, however, that this should not become an obsessive or spiraling behavior. The entire point of project management inversion is being objective, without attaching any negative self-talk to the potential outcomes you're running through. To do so, you could use a few techniques; perhaps, try talking it out with a person who is impartial to the task. Another suggestion, if you are susceptible to negativity, would be to create a list of both possible failures and possible successes to balance out your perspective.

Productivity

Applying inversion thinking to productivity is my personal favorite. Procrastination is a massive problem for a large part of the population. We live in a world where we are constantly inundated with fresh new content coming at us from all sources, so it's easy to get distracted.

When you apply inversion thinking to your productivity, the question becomes, "what if I wanted to decrease my focus?" As in, thinking about how you can become distracted, rather than how you can avoid it. The answers to those questions will help you determine the interruptions that you should eliminate to free up your focus for what you have to do. If you know you're a sucker for a phone notification, try putting it on mute. If that doesn't work, start putting it in another room or in a place that is too inconvenient to access often. Once you've mastered the small things, you can broaden this approach by thinking bigger. For example, if you're aware that you procrastinate due to wanting to spend time with your friends, put your mind at ease by scheduling your meetups ahead of time. Thinking your distractions through before starting your work, leaves little room for spontaneous disturbances.

This insight reveals a principle that is important to remember, especially for those of us who tend to dwell on fears and negative thoughts: While chasing success blindly can have big consequences, preventing failure often carries very little risk.

Decluttering

The best-seller *The Life-Changing Magic of Tidying Up* by Marie Kondo applies inversion thinking to help people declutter their homes. The author's standout line is that "we should be choosing what we want to keep, not what we want to get rid of." In other words, your default setting should be to give up anything which does not kindle joy in your life. I put this philosophy to good use myself when I was sorting out my garage a few years ago. It is incredible, the number of things we keep around, gathering dust, just because we can't bring ourselves to discard them.

To apply this to your own life, stop going through your belongings during spring cleaning, looking for garbage to throw out. Instead, go in with the objective of finding what you truly treasure as a belonging. With this method, you may end up getting rid of a lot more junk than with the opposite approach.

Relationships

It's been known for quite some time now that nearly half of all marriages in the United States end in divorce (Wilkinson & Finkbeiner, 2022). I have a few theories on why modern marriages tend to dissolve so often, with most of them hinging on either personal or societal expectations. For now, though, let's brainstorm some possible relationship factors— what can bring about the end of a marriage? Is it a lack of trust? Of respect? Not spending enough time with one another or not having enough communication? Inverting a good marriage (or any relationship, really) can show you how to avoid a bad one. We often don't notice our faults until they are pointed out to us. To prevent frustrating your partner with your unforeseen imperfections, think ahead—

could you be communicating with them better? Are you truly supporting them to the best of your abilities? This tactic of inversion simply shines a light on possible improvements before it's too late.

Personal Finance

Money: The cause of, and solution to, so many of life's problems. Debt accumulation, overspending, a lack of budgeting, and bad investments, are just a few factors that contribute to poor personal finances.

So, before you start worrying about how to earn more money, make sure you've figured out how not to lose it first. If you can manage to avoid that, you'll be ahead of most people, and ultimately save yourself a lot of anxiety. With personal finance, inversion thinking is pretty easy in theory: make an adequate budget; a budget that covers possible emergencies in addition to your wish list.

In conclusion, inversion thinking is a great way for you to reframe your negative thoughts, in order to apply them to something constructive. If your natural inkling is to always think of the worst-case scenario and stress about it, put your efforts toward finding solutions for it. Inversion thinking demonstrates perfectly why I was never supportive of stuffing down your negative thoughts in favor of artificial positive ones; instead, we have the capability of using negative thoughts to our ultimate benefit.

Personalized Solutions

Some people might wish that they could just take an antibiotic to rid themselves of pesky, negative thoughts. Unfortunately, there are no pills, supplements, or prescriptions that can cure your excessive negativity, like with a regular physical illness. Since the remedies are not as straightforward, each person is tasked with finding the best psychological solutions to fit their individual needs. What I mean, is that each of our brains functions uniquely and might require different approaches.

First, let's understand something called "neuroplasticity." Ultimately, the brain can change and adapt, proving that our thought processes, points of view, and habits are *not* set in stone. This fact directly contradicts people that say "oh, that's just the way I am," to explain a bad habit of theirs that they refuse to kick. In a way, yes, we do have some predetermined tendencies, however, they are never fixed. If there is something we want to change about the way we think, it's possible to do so more often than not.

There are two forms of neuroplasticity: functional plasticity and structural plasticity. The former corresponds to the brain's ability to reorganize its functions from a damaged part of the brain to a healthy one, while the latter is its ability to alter its physical structure.

What we'll be focusing on due to its relevance to this chapter, is called self-directed neuroplasticity. As the name indicates, this simply refers to when a person takes rewiring their brain into their own hands. How is this done? Often, through actively breaking a habit loop.

A habit loop is a cycle that explains why people partake in habits over and over again if they understand the damage it's causing them. Examples include checking your phone first thing in the morning, always stopping at a fast food drive-thru on your way home from work, leaving the dishes sitting in the sink to go do something else, etcetera. Why do we do all these things, knowing full well that they are hindering us? It's due to one vexing little habit loop composed of four parts:

1. **The cue.** The cue (also called the trigger) is what sets our habit loop into motion. It begins as soon as we notice a familiar environment, in which we tend to partake in a certain habit. For example, if you need to wash the dishes, your cue would be that you feel a sense of boredom rising up at the thought of actually doing it.

2. **The craving.** Once the cue is in motion, we instantly want to replace it with something more enjoyable. For the previous example, the sense of boredom from washing the dishes would make you instantly crave going to sit down on your couch and watch a show instead.

3. **The routine.** Following the call of the craving, we then partake in the habit that we've established by following through with what we truly want to do. You leave the dishes sitting in the sink once again and go to the couch. This is what leads to the fourth and last part of the habit loop.

4. **The reward.** Once we allow ourselves to partake in the habit, we are rewarded with feel-good hormones. This makes us feel satisfied for having followed our urges, rather than doing what we know is right. It is the release of these feel-good hormones that further reinforce our habits.

Notice-Shift-Rewire

The habit loop is directly related to the technique I'll describe in this sub-section. We now know that the feel-good hormones are so overpowering, that our brains lead us into making poor decisions over, and over, and over again. Habit loops are pretty much unavoidable if we don't take matters into our own hands.

The technique known as notice-shift-rewire is meant to help you break the habit loop of the negativity bias. Thankfully, it's a pretty straightforward process, but don't let its simplicity fool you—through dedication and repetition, it will get the job done, and your brain will mold itself to adapt to a new environment—one that doesn't allow it to default to excessive negativity. The following three steps make up this technique (Klemp, 2019):

1. **Take notice of the negativity bias**. This is perhaps the trickiest part to master, since we may be subjected to negativity bias so often that catching each instance is tough. This first step simply encourages you to be more mindful of your thoughts. If we experience rejection at work, for example, we need to bring attention to our thoughts if they mimic something like "I must not be good enough," or "my boss probably hates me." When these thoughts bombard your mind, take a second to reflect!

2. **Shift your mindset to something more positive: gratitude.** Once you've taken notice of your negativity bias, actively think of something that opposes it. If the automatic thought was "I

must not be good enough," list what you are grateful for regarding yourself, your skills, and the job you have. You may even feel a small weight being lifted off your chest as you prevent yourself from spiraling. Gratitude is also known as one of the most powerful tools for creating new, better neural pathways.

3. **Rewire your brain!** Seems easier said than done, right? Well, this step gets its name from what it achieves *over time*. Meaning, it isn't a one-time fix, but it is easy enough for you to do it often; all you have to do is savor the good in your life. Take what you did in step two, and apply it on a broader scale, or just to remember good moments from the past—anything that gets you to notice the significance of the positives of your life over the negatives. Spend 15 to 30 seconds thinking of the positives and you will be one step closer to solidly rewiring your brain.

CBT Made Easy

Cognitive Behavioral Therapy (CBT) is a form of psychotherapy that is highly effective in improving one's overall life quality. It covers a wide range of issues, including depression, anxiety, eating disorders, relationship issues, substance use, and more. Generally, it is performed as talk therapy with a professional psychologist but has a high success rate when done solo as well. CBT done alone allows you to be your own therapist; you learn your triggers and become equipped to deal with many psychological and or emotional issues thrown your way.

The next time you feel your anxiety flaring up or your negative thoughts clouding your judgment, you can sit down and get ready to write. CBT suggests that you do the following:

1. Assess your level of distress. Pick a number range that makes the most sense to you, such as 1 to 10, 0 to 100, or what I tend to choose for myself: 1 to 5. 1, for me, is a pretty relaxed state of being, while 5 indicates that I am actively being sucked into the void of negativity.

2. Next, make note of what had occurred to trigger this distress of yours. What thoughts automatically flooded your mind as soon as it happened? If you were set off by a low grade on an important exam, for example, think about what went through your mind as soon as you received the news. Was it, "I knew I would fail, why did I even try?" Or perhaps, "I am not made for this—I don't have the skillset"?

3. Think back to the categories of negative thinking presented in Chapter 3 and ask yourself if this reaction of yours exhibits one of the described types. Are you overgeneralizing by attaching too much importance to this one failure? Are you catastrophizing and feeling like your life is over because of this one fault? By knowing what type of negative thinking is occurring, you can begin to shift away from it.

4. Look for evidence that your emotional reaction to this trigger is not objective. If you are feeling like you don't have the skill set to ever pass this exam, what points to this being untrue? For example, you might have spent weeks preparing for this exam,

proving that you *were* building up your knowledge for this exam; or, maybe you passed all the practice exams and were simply overcome with some nasty test anxiety that caused you to fail the official one.

5. Imagine you are a different person who is having a conversation with you about the situation. If you told your best friend that you are not intelligent enough to pass this exam, what would they say? If they're a good friend, they would most likely point out all of the reasons why you should not be feeling this way. Imagine what they would say—this forces you to take another perspective.

6. Using the previous steps, reconsider what happened, and reevaluate the severity of the situation without any cognitive distortions. You could ask yourself: Will this matter to me in two years? Chances are, your negativity bias has temporarily made you forget about the rest of your life's successes.

7. Write down your thoughts and feelings on the event from a more objective standpoint, such as, "failing this exam made me feel disappointed, given how much time I spent preparing for it." The sentence shouldn't use any false positivity, but rather, just be an objective statement of your feelings.

8. Using the same scale as before, give a new score to how anxious, depressed, or otherwise distressed you feel.

CBT takes practice and commitment. Many people choose to start with doing this exercise several times per day before toning it down to less. Although CBT may seem like a short-term fix that applies to issues on a very individual basis, the repetition of it leads to the rewiring of your brain away from extreme negativity.

Key Points

Let's look over the most important takeaways from Chapter 6:

- Inversion thinking is kind of like applying reverse psychology to avoid negativity: it helps us take on another perspective and become more objective
- Inversion thinking can be applied to any area in which you feel like you struggle with overwhelming negativity
- Feeding into bad negative habits causes them to get stronger—if we do not make the effort to break them, we fail to move forward
- Notice-shift-rewire is a technique used to toss your brain out of a state of negativity, and with enough repetition, it may replace the habit of negativity
- CBT is a powerful form of self-therapy to provide a different perspective on a negatively-perceived situation

Chapter 7
Finding the Light at the End of the Tunnel

"Happiness is a direction, not a place."

— Sydney J. Harris

A lot of methods I will suggest for transforming your negative thinking don't have much to do with negativity at all. Instead, most of the heavy work will come directly from improving *other* areas of your life. A person who allows themselves to be happy and actively tries to enjoy their life is significantly less susceptible to being seized by negativity. For this chapter, I'll ask you to shift your focus to your life in general. We'll be exploring how strongly emotions intertwine with your outlook on life, changes you can make to improve your life's satisfaction, and the difference some simple lifestyle changes can make.

Emotions: Guilty or Innocent?

If you think back to the content in Chapter 2 regarding changes in mindset throughout history, you'll recall reading about the Romanticism era—a period full of art with subjective meaning and emotional expression. This was crucial in our development as a global society, as it was finally allowing us to focus on the value of immaterial aspects of life. This was precisely what psychologist Abraham Harold Maslow was exploring when he made the five-tiered pyramid called "Maslow's Hierarchy of Needs" (McLeod, 2020). This pyramid is meant to show what needs people focus on, according to the level of their necessity for survival and or life. For example, the bottom (and largest) section of the pyramid is physiological needs, such as food, water, and shelter. This means that these parts of life are the most essential for survival, and without them, most people wouldn't be focused on needs placed higher up on the pyramid. The top three tiers of the pyramid—belongingness and love, esteem, and self-actualization—are the ones that society had started to focus on, initiated during the Romanticism era. Unlike the bottom two tiers—physiological needs and safety needs—the top three are focused on emotional and mental elements. This goes to show that while we think of physical things as being essential for survival, attending to emotional needs is essential for *happiness*.

Now, to be clear, happiness will not erase your negative thinking, and nor should it. It does, however, prevent negative thinking from taking over your life.

So far, research has shown that the amygdala in happier people had the same level of activity when shown joyful images as it did when the individual was shown sad images

(Allen & Smith, 2016). This alone is enough to indicate that happy people don't retain their positivity by ignoring the bad in their life, but simply that they attach an equal amount of importance to both the bad and the good. In happy people, the negativity bias is not triumphant—it is balanced out by how carefully they try to experience the good.

Making Time for What Counts

Time is in limited supply for us all. "Time is money," as Ben Franklin said (1748); but, I would argue that time isn't money—it's happiness.

We all dedicate time to what matters to us. To some, spending 60 hours per week at work satisfies their need to feel accomplished or wealthy; to others, spending a month traveling every year feels non-negotiable. Time is valuable because it's a limited resource that dictates how good we feel. Think of a day where nothing seems to be going right— your work took two more hours to complete than you expected, you were too tired to go to the event you were looking forward to, and you were too down in the dumps to do anything beyond binge watch a show. Chances are that the following day you might feel like the previous day was wasted since you didn't get to spend your time in a way that brought you joy. So, applying this to your everyday life, what should you do to avoid this feeling?

Time management is the answer, but it might not be what you are used to. When people are told to make a timetable for their day, many run to fill up their schedules to the brim, making productivity the goal. But should it be? What if the goal, instead, was satisfaction? This satisfaction does not have to be a surface-level guilty pleasure, but rather, it should include your work, your relaxation, and your progress. How much time do you need to spend on each of these to truly be satisfied with your day?

Burnout does not discriminate—it is the sense of extreme exhaustion, dullness, loss of passion, and even possibly depression. It creeps up on you bit by bit while you are out there, working passionately, thinking you are about to sprint to the finish line of success. Burnout is the unpleasant reminder that the journey to success should be treated like a marathon, instead. Being blinded by motivation or a passionate drive, we often lose sight of the fact that our time has to be divided more evenly. The true satisfaction of time management comes from this exact balance.

So, when I suggest that you time manage, I don't want you to go making a 30-point essential to-do list, working yourself to the bone. You should be dedicating your time to things you truly enjoy as well: spending time with loved ones, going outdoors, partaking in a hobby (no matter how silly), and overall, just taking time for yourself. This is a step to solidify your dedication to noticing the good.

A Shift in Mental Focus

When thinking of happiness, we need to remember one thing: we will always want more. There's a reason why most people think, "why don't billionaires just stop earning money?" Well, I can think of a few explanations, but the most accurate one is that they are not satisfied with what they already have. Crazy, right? Having 10 billion dollars only makes them want to make 10 billion more! To the average joe, 10 billion dollars is something we will never see, so to want 20 billion dollars seems simply ridiculous; and yet, this doesn't work in the psychology of a billionaire.

Humans have a very weird and confusing relationship between chasing after desires and feeling satisfied with achieving said desires. What we can get from this is key to understanding our journey toward happiness: it isn't a destination. A crucial thing to understand to be happy is that obtaining the things we desire is not enough in itself to make us happy—we have to find additional avenues.

Growing Your Self-Confidence

People walk a fine line when it comes to their relationship with themselves. On one end of the spectrum, they might be struggling to not see a failure in the mirror; on the other, they may feel like a God among men. Ego is something we all have, but not a lot of us understand exactly what it is or how to deal with it. Too much or too little of an ego is enough to ruin your life, just like the wrong amount of baking soda would do to a cake.

So, what is ego? Is it Narcissus, falling deeply in love with his reflection? Is it that irksome, guilt-filled satisfaction that arises when you realize you are doing better in life than those around you?

The word "ego" is Latin for the word "I," but it gets more complicated than that. In psychology, the concept of the human ego came into play when famous psychologist Sigmund Freud introduced it in the early 20th century. He explained it as a complicated part of ourselves that melds together our animalistic and moral tendencies, but nowadays, many people confuse ego with confidence. However, the difference becomes quite clear with a simple explanation.

Ego is when someone believes they deserve or will attain things simply because of who they are. Self-confidence, however, is believing they will attain things based on their objective merits, such as working hard for them. Compare the phrase, "I don't even have to try to get it," with the phrase, "I deserve to get it because I have been putting in the work." One exhibits a blind belief in yourself based solely on who you are, and the other is based on the conscious actions you made.

Self-esteem is kind of the best of both worlds from ego and self-confidence: It is how much we value ourselves, even if we are in a productivity slump. Low self-esteem often starts in childhood when you feel as if you are a disappointment to your loved ones or unable to meet their or your expectations. Self-esteem is further lowered when people are stuck in a negative mindset. Catastrophizing, overgeneralization, personalization, and minimizing all continuously contribute toward beating down your self-esteem. While these negative types of thinking continue, healthy self-esteem is extremely hard to achieve.

What you need to do to be happier is have a balanced ego, a healthy self-esteem, and lots of self-confidence. Easier said than done though, no? Well, luckily, there are several practical methods for you to try.

Be kind to yourself

If you've ever done some prior research on reframing negative thinking, I'm sure you've heard this one before. The difference is, I'll tell you precisely what I did to eventually achieve this colossal task. When I had stretches of difficult times in my 20s, I struggled a lot with my self-esteem. I tried many things, with very few results. It wasn't until I was completely fed up with feeling bad about myself that I took some radical steps.

First, I forced myself to be kind to myself—and I did this quite literally. Every morning, I would look in the mirror for one to two minutes straight, before coming up with at least five compliments to give myself. Instead of choosing things I hated about myself and pretending like I liked them, I challenged myself to find aspects I truly felt good about. This made me discover that there *were* many things I liked about myself, but they got buried under the massive pile of my 'flaws.'

Within a few weeks of that exercise, I found a new objective for myself: to get comfortable with being uncomfortable. During that period of my life, I was a much smaller person —personality-wise. I felt truly myself when I wasn't worried about someone else's judgment. So, I decided to do things I perceived would make me feel embarrassed. For example, if I liked my outfit but was tempted to not wear it out of fear that others would think it looked bad, I wore that outfit. It was incredibly challenging at first and even emotionally tolling. However, when I would get home that night, I felt incredible; it made me realize that nothing *truly* bad happened just because I felt a little bit less conventional. Suddenly, the catastrophizing thoughts melted away; I eventually became unfazed by others' judgment—if they didn't like me, I no longer felt like I was an entirely bad person.

Practice being assertive

There are a lot of people who confuse assertiveness with a lack of tact. In my opinion, however, being honest with yourself and the other person is the most respectful thing you can do. If you are invited to an outing you know you don't want to go to, saying "no" does not necessarily mean you do not value them or their offer.

Assertiveness is an essential component of self-respect, and consequently, self-esteem. When we respect our time, our wishes, and our desires—all without sacrificing them to please others—we are inherently honoring our values. Saying "no" when needed is important to practice to increase your assertiveness, but it is not the only way. I would recommend thinking of it more as decreasing your passiveness, rather than increasing your assertiveness—at least, at first. If your coworker interrupts you with their idea, practice not being passive by speaking up and saying some-thing like "excuse me, I'd appreciate it if I could just finish the point I was making." To someone who makes them-selves smaller to appease others, this phrase might even seem rude or brash. In reality, it does not contain any disre-spectful language.

Assertiveness also requires you to stop being constantly self-less. If you struggled to impress your family as a child, you might overcompensate now by doing the absolute most you can for everybody around you. To change this, treat your time as sacred. In the previous section of this chapter, we talked about prioritizing rest to prevent burnout. Now, we combine that with the notion that your time is yours, no matter how you choose to spend it.

Personally, I have a very firm rule: I will always make sure I have time to myself and will not sacrifice it for someone else unless I want to make that change or it is an emergency. If I made a firm plan to spend two hours working and one hour resting, I kindly say "no" to someone asking me to help them with something trivial during that particular time block. I value my time, my schedule, and the fact that I need both time to work and time to rest. Prioritizing your time is not selfish for you nor me—you cannot help someone when you yourself are struggling, so make your life the priority.

Setting boundaries

There's a reason that assertiveness was discussed above because you will certainly need to get comfortable with it to set boundaries. Setting boundaries is one of the most under-rated and overlooked methods of ensuring healthy relation-ships; not just with romantic partners, but friendships, family members, and even coworkers. Due to them being often overlooked, many people don't even realize why some of their relationships are so draining.

Boundaries are an extremely personal thing. Some people have boundaries that we do not understand and vice versa. However, whether we understand them or not, they deserve respect. Oftentimes, someone establishing a boundary is a sign that they *want* to keep you in your life and not the opposite. So, think of boundaries as tools to ensure mutually respectful relationships.

Sometimes, people who drain us in one way or another are not of ill intent. Many of them may not even notice the effects of their actions. If someone is used to you saying "yes" to everything they ask of you, they will likely continue to unassumingly do so. For a time-draining relationship as such, you could establish a boundary by starting the conversation with something like, "I really value my own time, and from now on, I will only be available when my schedule and energy level allow it." If your counterpart reacts poorly to your boundaries, it is an indication that they profited from you not having any in the first place. The only relationships worth keeping are those where you both strive to be better for each other and respect each other's needs.

Key Points

Let's look over the most important takeaways from Chapter 7:

- As long as basic survival requirements are met, people achieve happiness through emotional fulfillment
- Time is a precious and limited resource—the things you spend time on are the ones that will be nourished the most
- People are meant to want more and more, failing to be satisfied with what we already have; don't assume you'll be happy forever once you achieve a certain milestone
- Self-confidence is required for true happiness and success—develop it by going outside of your comfort zone, being conscious of your thoughts, and don't be afraid to put yourself first

Chapter 8
Think Lovely Thoughts?

"Mindfulness isn't difficult. We just need to remember to do it."

— Sharon Salzberg

Positive thinking is so celebrated in mainstream media that it has become this sort of mantra for millions of people around the world. Everyone promotes it, from self-help gurus to Instagram influencers, and we all take it in as something we should be doing more of in our day-to-day. The problem is that positive thinking is generally said to operate by canceling out negative thoughts—which is something that's never going to work. Our negative thoughts will keep coming to us, and they don't deserve to be seen as this threat that needs to be vanquished. If we try to push them out instead of dealing with them accordingly, it would be the same as trying to push a plastic ball underwater—the moment we let go, it will shoot its way back to the surface.

Besides, it's no help to tell yourself you don't feel a certain way when you do. My go-to example is always the finger cut: If you're in the kitchen and you cut yourself, then saying you're not wounded won't make the cut disappear, you still need to tend to it or there might be an infection, making things much worse.

In the context of positivity, trying to mask your negative thoughts can occur when you get the gut feeling that you don't like someone you've met. Say you're in a social setting and someone there is just giving you an icky vibe. Positive thinking essentially tells you not to humor those feelings and to instantly force yourself to like them, but it may very well be that your intuition is right and the person poses a threat to you. It would be of help to try and figure out why you feel something is wrong with that person. In reality, it could very well be that you simply don't like the way they are dressing or the number of tattoos they have, which might reveal some sort of inner prejudice within you that you could work on—it's always great when we recognize that there is room for growth within us! But maybe it will also make you watch your back, keep your belongings near you, and keep a close eye on the drinks you are served. Unless you have a direct problem with anxiety or paranoia, that icky feeling from the beginning may very well be saving you at times.

So, to sum it up, the key to handling negative thoughts is to acknowledge them, try to get to the root of why you are having them, and then react accordingly. In this chapter, I'll be introducing you to another key component of handling negative thoughts and preventing negativity bias: mindfulness.

How Mindfulness Fits Into Your Life

"Mindfulness" is a word that gets tossed around a lot nowadays. It gets tossed around not only by influencers trying to be relevant in the modern trend of caring for mental health but even by companies. Corporations and businesses have noticed this shift in mentality toward an emphasis on being present and mentally healthy. With this information, many of them have started to do something I like to call "mindfulness-washing" (originating from the idea of "green-washing"); they will pretend to be mindful to gain respect, attention, and new clients. This is quite literally the opposite of what mindfulness is meant for.

In the simplest of terms, mindfulness is about being present in the world around you. It originated in the Buddhist and Hindu religions that were briefly described in the second chapter. This ancient practice has no better time to be gaining popularity than right now, however. With so much of our lives revolving around money, social media, and technology, we often lose sight of what else we have around us. Even most jobs nowadays will have you staring at your computer screen for seven to eight hours a day. While you do this, the world still turns, the sun still shines, the wind still blows, and you might be forgetting about all of these pleasantries.

Mindfulness is a large component of Zen Buddhism—a branch of original Buddhism. Whether you are religious or spiritual in some capacity or not, mindfulness is a practice that goes beyond just its traditional objective of enlightenment. In today's world, it's used largely to give your brain a rest and to prevent burnout, since it slows your pace down.

The Effects of Mindfulness

Neuroscientist Zoran Josipovic believes that there are two networks in the brain: the extrinsic network and the intrinsic (default) network (Danzico, 2011). The former is responsible for focusing our attention on the external world, such as things we see or tasks we have to complete. The latter is in charge of focusing our attention on our internal world, such as thinking about ourselves and how we feel. However, these two networks are rarely equipped at the same time; instead, when one is really active, the other is barely functional. This would explain why people feel out of touch with themselves when they're stressed with work: their intrinsic network hasn't gotten to be active in a long time. Thankfully, mindfulness is supposed to provide us with a balance of the two.

In today's society, mindfulness is treated as optional; lots of people in the West don't see it as an important part of their lives. I didn't either, at first. We aren't exactly taught what mindfulness is in school or seminars, so I never heard about it until I was in my late 20s. To be honest, I didn't feel like it would make much of a difference in my thought process, but I tried it anyway because it seemed like a quick way to relax. I was both right and wrong; mindfulness does have an instant short-term effect on you in the form of relaxation, but it started to provide me with much more. I eventually started being mindful even when I didn't consciously make the choice to be. It became an ingrained habit that I easily applied to my entire life. Soon, I saw the most significant change it caused: I no longer felt as if life was zooming right past me—I started experiencing every day of my life. My days weren't a blur, my hours didn't pass me by, and I started to feel as if the things I spent my time and energy on were benefiting my journey.

I could go on and on about how important mindfulness is, but I'm sure the more useful approach to convince you of its significance is to present some proof. Well, scientific studies have shown that mindfulness has effects on several parts of the brain that span functions such as perception, complex thought processes, emotional management, introspection, pain tolerance, and sense of self (Congleton et al., 2016). At least four of those (complex thinking, emotional management, introspection, and sense of self) are highly beneficial to our cause of increasing positivity. When these four improve, we stop being as susceptible to anxiety, stress, and the negativity bias—all because our minds are stronger in resistance to negativity.

Another study was tasked with taking brain scans of people who meditate regularly. The researchers ended up scanning the brain of a Buddhist monk four times, with many years passing in between each scan. What they concluded from their last scan during which the monk was 41 years old, was that his brain appeared to have aged only 33 years—an entire eight years younger (Geggel, 2020). This acts as proof that things such as mindfulness, and therefore meditation, can physically improve the way our brains function.

Inhale, Exhale...

Mindfulness is all about acceptance, not change—similar to what I've been proposing throughout this book: don't *mask* your negative thoughts, *use* them. Accepting is all about opening up to your inner experiences, such as your thoughts and feelings. It involves an active and aware embrace of said experiences as they emerge, and allowing them to be present rather than attempting to change, minimize, or avoid them.

The most well-known approach to the practice of mindfulness and awareness is meditation. The core principle of all types of meditation boils down to accepting the external world and simply observing what you have going on inside. They generally start with you sitting or lying down, getting in touch with your body and your five senses, and then noticing your thoughts and emotions. With your eyes closed and your focus on your breath and body, the thoughts that are most important to you at that time will eventually pop up. Rather than getting frustrated that instead of ascending into some spiritual realm you are thinking about daily stresses, you let them be—you allow your mind to run its course. Anxiety is often caused by a whirlpool of emotions brought up by a thought, and the stronger we fight against it, the more violent it becomes. Meditation allows you to approach your mind as a neutral entity by allowing it to simply experience whatever it wants, without judgment.

Meditation is not the only approach to mindfulness, however. Although I am a big advocate of incorporating meditation into your everyday life, sometimes other techniques are better for beginners. The great thing about mindfulness is that ultimately, it is not an activity or an exercise—it is a lifestyle and a thought process; it may start as an exercise before spilling into every corner of your life. For this reason, I'd like to introduce a few non-meditative means of increasing your mindfulness.

Journaling

The first is journaling. Now, there is not just one way to journal—there are a limitless number of things that you can write. The type of journaling I'm referring to, however, is narrowed down to a few key points: getting in touch with your present self.

When I first started journaling, I would carry around a small journal almost everywhere I went. Whenever I felt overwhelmed, anxious, or any other unpleasant emotion, I would take it out and put all my thoughts down on paper. Nowadays, I've reduced my journaling to once per day, as soon as I wake up. If you are a morning person (or are trying to be) I recommend you do the same.

Keep a notebook and pen on your bedside table, and make this the centerpiece. When you first wake up, whatever you do, do not look at your phone. You might want to take five or so minutes to yourself, doing a mental run-through of your upcoming day, before reaching over and getting to some mindful work. If you want a structure, you could write down your thoughts or worries in bullet-point format and then provide a few phrases for each one, explaining why you feel that way. If you're like me and you prefer ultimate creative freedom, follow the 'stream of consciousness' technique. For this, the steps are very easy: Write down whatever you are thinking, no matter how much sense you think it might make or how pretty it looks. Allow your mind to throw itself onto the pages, making your feelings seem less than undefeatable. For some reason, seeing the way you feel written down in front of you can automatically make it seem more manageable.

Conversation

Who doesn't like spending a nice evening with the people whose company you enjoy the most? Hopefully not you, because for this next mindfulness technique, you'll need a casual conversation partner.

Just like journaling, there are not many rules here for you to follow. All I ask is that you listen to what the other person is saying while they are saying it. Easy, right? Well actually, many people don't realize how easy it is for us to think about ourselves even while we listen to others. More particularly, people tend to automatically start thinking of their response to what is being said to them before the person has even finished talking. On one hand, yes, you're prepared to continue the conversation. On the other hand, however, you may be failing to truly soak up the meaning of your conversational partner's words.

The next time you're talking to someone, focus all of your attention on them. What is their tone? Does their choice of words alter what they are saying? What is their body language like? Not only does this allow you to fully immerse yourself in the conversation from the other person's perspective, but you are solidifying your experience in the present moment—all that mindfulness is about.

Eating

"Mindful eating"—maybe you've heard of it, maybe you know someone who's tried it, but what is it exactly, and does it work?

The short answer is yes, it works. Mindful eating is a very easy concept to understand. What stops most people from using it is that it seems time-consuming. Ironic, though, isn't it? Anyone who wants to be more mindful of themselves and their thoughts should be trying to *escape* from the idea that everything has to happen as quickly as possible.

Mindful eating is similar to that of mindful conversation: You try to notice as much as possible. The twist, in this case, is that you must try to apply all your five senses.

Grab a bowl of food for your dinner and before consuming it all in front of the TV, try to do something different. First, take a look at it: How many colors can you count? Are there different shades of each color? What do you think the textures will feel like on your tongue? Then, apply your sense of smell; what are the smells you are experiencing? Does the smell remind you of anything? You can continue to ask similar questions as you go through every one of your five senses; is the plate of food hot to the touch? How many flavors can you taste? Does the food make any particular sound when you chew it or touch it with your utensil?

Many people go beyond their senses when doing mindful eating. In particular, they like to think about where the ingredients came from. As you take each bite, try to think of the origins of an ingredient in the food. Perhaps they originated halfway across the world, or maybe you grew it yourself in the backyard.

It is only through such laser focus that you can begin to honor your food, and therefore honor your relationship with it in the present moment.

Thinking Intentional Thoughts

Some people fail to realize the solid connection between mindfulness and negative thoughts. After all, what does the sound my food makes have anything to do with my anxiety? To answer that, we have to understand that every action we take, impacts our thought processes. This is not meant to scare you into over-analyzing everything you do or expect yourself to be perfect, but to think about the general trend of your actions. So yes, even paying attention to your meal or writing down your emotions once per day can end up making a large impact on how you view life, and therefore, the negativity bias.

Cognitive Defusion

This process complements your efforts to be mindful and to stop judging yourself for your thoughts and emotions; it requires you to take a step back, distance yourself from your thoughts, memories, and images, and objectively notice them as they are. This prevents you from attributing to them a label of any kind (such as "negative" or "painful").

There are three good ways to do this:

- "Just noticing": When you start having a negative thought, acknowledge it by saying, for example, "I notice I'm having the thought that I'm useless, again. That's the third time today."
- "Thanking the mind": When you take a moment to sarcastically give your mind appreciation for the unhelpful thought it ushered in, it helps you to realize just how silly the thought is, and that your original reaction to it was even sillier; this, effectively, takes away its power. "Ah, thanks a lot, brain, for making me feel useless for the third time today."
- "Repeating a thought": Interestingly enough, repeating a negative thought over and over again might make you realize that you have no reason to listen to it. If you repeat your thought out loud,

especially if you do it in a funny voice or even by singing it, it will help you create more distance from it.

Key Points

Let's look over the most important takeaways from Chapter 8:

- You cannot treat negativity as if it does not exist—don't shy away from acknowledging your tendencies
- Our relationship with the present moment is key in preventing the negativity bias from taking over
- Mindfulness is the practice of solidifying yourself in the present moment and treating what goes on in your mind as neutral
- Mindfulness can and should be applied to many areas of your life—meditation is a great technique for mindfulness, but it is not the only one
- The concept of cognitive defusion allows us to disconnect from our pesky, negative thoughts through three different possible techniques

Chapter 9
Seeking Motivation

"You are never too old to set another goal or to dream a new dream."

— C.S Lewis

Negativity can zap everything enjoyable about life right out of it. Your passions, your interests, your hopes, your dreams, and your curiosity, to name a few. Another key component of life that falls victim to ravenous negativity, is motivation.

Motivation is the bread and butter of our enjoyment of life. It differs for each of us and steers us into individual paths, but without it, life can become quite dull; projects that you used to look forward to no longer seem interesting; the hobbies you wanted to try pursuing have transformed into simple time-wasters that you don't see the point for. When things that are meant to give you an interest in life are lost, you may become disappointed in yourself. Losing your motivation can become a very slippery slope to an unsatis-factory life or even, possibly, depression.

Excited, Not Afraid

There are two types of people in the world: those who are intimidated by unpredictability and those who are inspired by it. Neither group is wrong, since unpredictability can exhibit both factors; however, one group is certainly being a little held back by their perspective.

I always say that the most predictable thing about life is that it will always be unpredictable. We can always count on it to throw in surprises that we are expected to deal with (both good and bad). The way we feel in anticipation of these surprises can either set us up for success or failure. Your negative thoughts and the way you expect to handle life's surprises have a clear relationship: with unwanted nega-tivity comes pessimism or doubt that you will be able to handle the future.

In this chapter, we will be revolving around an ideology I presented in Chapter 7: getting comfortable with being uncomfortable. In fact, that's really all there is to it! The bottom line is that we have to stop treating unpredictability as a threat and start viewing it as a gift.

Growth vs Fixed Mindset

To look forward to challenges and even enjoy them, you need to have a belief instilled in yourself; the belief is that you will be able to not only handle all of life's future chal-lenges flowing down the current, but that you will grow from them. For this belief to come to life, you will have to possess a growth mindset.

At its essence, a growth mindset is all about promoting effort, not perfection. It is not the expectation of yourself to instantaneously master every skill you set your eyes on, but rather that by applying yourself, you could make quite a bit of progress. A person with a growth mindset does not shy away from challenges because they believe that, regardless of their success, they are improving their skills. A growth mindset suggests they believe that through determination and effort, their skills and talents are capable of being improved and that they are not static.

At the other end of the spectrum, we have the concept of a fixed mindset. As the name suggests, people with a fixed mindset lack the belief that they can truly alter what they are good at. Instead, they believe that their skills and talents are more innate than anything and that challenging tasks are simply not meant for them.

Interestingly, we are all combinations of the two mindsets. If you've ever given up on something simply because it's "too hard," you've exhibited a fixed mindset. On the contrary, if you've ever put in the effort to learn something completely new to you, you've exhibited a growth mindset. A perfect growth mindset doesn't exist, as we all have both inside of us. The difference lies in the mindset we mostly rely on when faced with a challenge.

A growth mindset is more useful for absolutely any endeavor. With this perspective, you are facing the challenge head-on. Most people who exhibit this type of mindset achieve more than those who have a fixed mindset. This is not because they have better skills or anything like that, but simply because they try more new things and boldly attempt demanding tasks. After all, if you cast a wider net, you will likely get more fish!

Working On Growth

Another key component of a growth mindset that I haven't mentioned yet is accepting failure; not only that, but actively learning from your failure. If you are someone who gets intimidated by challenges quite often, you will want to learn how to transform your mindset into a growth-based one. I recommend the following useful tips on how to do so:

- Try something you've often told yourself you probably couldn't do. Maybe you've wanted to learn another language, but the magnitude of such a task scares you away from starting; or, maybe you've been wanting to start your own business. Wherever your desires may lie, it's time to let them out of their cages. It's scary, it's adrenaline-inducing, and it's inspiring, but at the end of the day, it will be worth it. So, take one small task you've been putting off because it slightly scares you, and vow to dive into it on a particular day.

- Do something badly and embrace it. This automatically goes against human nature—we don't actively strive for failure; but for the sake of your new-and-improved growth mindset, let's do exactly that. Think of an activity that you are aware you are bad at. It could be something like playing a sport, cooking a meal, writing an article, etcetera. Then, once you've done it, present it to someone for objective criticism. If you let go of your attachment to praise and validation, you open yourself up to learning from your mistakes. Starting with something simple begins training your mind to be more open to it, even on a larger scale.

- Redefine your idea of success. What is success to you? Do you have to do something near-perfectly to think of it as a success? If so, you are setting yourself up for disappointment. With a growth mindset, success is considered pure effort. By evaluating what it means to be successful to you, you might be able to change your perspective of success to include failures.

Rising to the Occasion

In many situations, success is a choice. I won't generalize and say that this is true for everyone, as there exists a lot of inequality in our society, but for many people, this should ring true. The reason so many people seemingly end up choosing wrong is because somewhere deep down, they might actually be afraid of success.

What makes a person scared of success? Well, first of all, realizing you're scared of success is not easy. Usually, it manifests as self-sabotage; an unwillingness to go after what you want, minimizing your skills and achievements. The reasons for this fear are vast, ranging from a lack of confidence to a sense of being undeserving of true success.

The first step toward overcoming something like this is breaking your history of self-sabotage, but that requires a keen sense of responsibility, and not being afraid to take accountability. Let's say you got an interview for a high-profile job that you used to wish for, but as the date for it approaches nearer and nearer, you still haven't begun preparing. Then, you wake up the day of the interview and quickly study the company and possible interview questions, just a couple of hours before. If you ended up feeling unprepared during the interview and did not get the job offer in the end, what are you blaming it on? Did you truly have no time to prepare, or was it unconscious self-sabotage pushing you to procrastinate?

If it's the latter, the truth might be a hard pill to swallow—your fear of success prevented you from believing in yourself and doing your best. However, it's better to recognize these faults and take full accountability so you prevent yourself from falling next time.

Increasing Motivation

Now, let's get to the fun part: sparking your motivation for life again. First of all, let's be clear that your zest for life comes from the motivation you have for different parts of it. In other words, you should be striving for motivation in many areas, including health, education, career, hobbies, travel, and so on.

Listening to inspiration

Inspiration often comes from other people. If there's someone you admire in a certain field, you can make a connection and ask them for some tips. If there's no one like that in your personal life, you're in luck—the internet is right at your fingertips!

I have become a massive fan of podcasts. I used to not understand the excitement of listening to people have casual conversations for half an hour or more, but then I found some that were right up my alley. I discovered podcasts about my hobbies, such as traveling, about improving mental health, career changes, and more. There are a lot of creative and successful people out there, so give them a listen! Not only does their success have the power to inspire you to want the same, but their experiences can allow you to get some additional knowledge about how to go about it.

Reading content

Reading is truly powerful. Although it has lost some of its popularity due to social media and other forms of content, its benefits have not decreased. If you could muster up the attention span, you could go all-in on a book. If you prefer something a little quicker to comb through, articles, blogs, and websites can present you with useful information in a very concise format.

Reading is always more enjoyable if you truly believe you're getting something out of it, whether that be entertainment or education.

Setting goals

When you set goals for yourself, your emotional reaction is a very telling thing. If you feel inspired when writing down your goals, you are on the right path. However, if you loathe the items on your list, perhaps it's time to make a change of path.

The method I recommend using for goal-setting is called SMART. This acronym stands for the following elements of a properly-set goal (Boogaard, 2021):

- **Specific.** A good goal diminishes vagueness as much as possible. Think about exactly what needs to be done for this goal to be achieved, and write it

down. What smaller steps must be accomplished
for you to get there? List everything required for
this goal to become a reality.

- **Measurable.** How will you be measuring your
progress? Perhaps consider a set amount of
progress you want to complete toward the goal at
equal intervals of time. You should have
benchmarks in place to keep track of your journey.

- **Achievable.** Let's be honest, some of us want too
much, too fast. So, for this bullet point, it's time for
a reality check: Can this be done? Do you have all
the materials that are required for this goal? No
one is saying that setting big goals is bad, but they
must be realistic.

- **Relevant.** Now, evaluate how you truly feel
about this goal. If you believe it will benefit your
life and make you happier, then it's worth the
effort. Make sure it aligns with your vision, your
desires, and your values.

- **Time-bound.** A goal without an end date is
simply a dream. To hold yourself accountable, set
a realistic date by which you would want to
achieve this goal. It can be a few weeks, months, or
even years in the future.

All-in-all, motivation is a powerful tool to say goodbye to
negativity bias. Without it, your negativity will get the best
of you and hold you back. Things such as goal-setting, inspiration, and taking risks are all aligned with the perspective
of someone who leads a positive life. Positive people
embrace what life gives them with a clear mind and a heart
full of passion.

Key Points

Let's look over the most important takeaways from Chapter 9:

- Our fear of being bad at something prevents us from trying and possibly succeeding
- Embracing the unpredictability of life will automatically boost your optimism
- A growth mindset is the belief that you can expand your skill set through effort
- A fixed mindset is the belief that your skill set is basically set in stone
- Becoming more open to the possibilities of the future means stepping out of your comfort zone
- Being afraid of success leads to self-sabotage, whether it's subtle or not
- Having a motivation for your life increases your satisfaction with it and consequently, your positivity

Chapter 10
Shadow Work for the Mind

"When we are aware of our weaknesses or negative tendencies, we open the opportunity to work on them."

— Allan Lokos

The most common solution we hear to mental health issues is therapy. Not only that, but therapy is also meant to help us through slumps, relationship issues, and problems with the way we view the world and ourselves. But, what do we do if we don't have the money for it? After all, therapy may be quite popular nowadays, but that doesn't make it any less expensive.

It's not that shadow work can replace therapy (nor should it), but it is a good alternative for someone who wants to get to the root of their issues without breaking the bank. The lack of a licensed professional present certainly makes this process a little less straightforward, but with enough honesty and vulnerability, shadow work's benefits are immeasurable.

Carl Jung—the famed Swiss psychologist—was the first to develop the concept of the shadow. He described it as the combination of repressed ideas, weaknesses, desires, instincts, and shortcomings (Cherry, 2022). The shadow is a part of all of us and is all of our ugly parts—our dark side. This part of ourselves isn't just one that we try to hide from others, but ourselves as well. Oftentimes, our shadow self can exhibit greed, envy, rage, hate, and prejudice; but, even if we don't like it, it's still there. Carl Jung believed that the shadow can show up in our dreams as various scary creatures such as snakes, demons, and dragons.

What's more interesting, however, is that the shadow self only gets bigger and stronger the longer we try to repress it. Otherwise, without coming to terms with our shadow, we allow it to make up a bigger part of ourselves. Accepting our shadow selves is no easy feat, in fact, when I first started doing shadow work, I was emotionally exhausted—but it was so worth it.

As you might've caught on, shadow work is tapping into those obscured parts of us, to establish a deeper connection to ourselves. This allows us to see ourselves for exactly who we are and why we think the way we do. Its benefits include:

- **Improved interactions with others.** The more self-aware you become, the more you trust yourself, and that kind of consciousness can be used in your relationships. For example, perhaps you were told as a child not to talk back to people, so you have trouble standing up for yourself as an adult. By doing shadow work, you can hone your boundaries and start to speak your truth.

- **Healing generational trauma.** A lot of people's families suffered terrible situations in the past that influenced generation after generation. To break this cycle, a person has to have a very strong sense of who they are and what they have to unlearn.

- **Learning healthy ways to meet your needs.** Our shadow selves can cause us to indulge in destructive behavior. For example, if a person's shadow holds within itself the idea that wanting closeness with someone is 'clingy,' they are more likely to cheat on their partner. Through shadow work, you can identify the desires that have been manifesting in harmful behavior.

- **Gaining confidence in yourself.** Shadow work allows us to come to terms with who we are—both the good and the bad. When we become aware of our mental shortcomings, we can come to accept them and nourish them with healthy alternatives. This, in turn, gets rid of our self-doubt that an ugly side of us will come out when we least expect it. Knowing who you truly are benefits your self-esteem.

- **Improved creativity.** Your shadow doesn't just hide traits of your personality, but also skills and inclinations you may have repressed because at some point in your life you were told they shouldn't be pursued. Accepting your shadow allows you to start authentically tapping into what you truly desire.

- **Increased mental clarity.** Overall, shadow work can help you understand your thoughts, emotions, and desires. Knowing your tendencies and 'ugly' parts helps you avoid them when needed.

Ignoring your shadow self is repression. Unfortunately, not coming to terms with it can lead to issues such as:

- Substance abuse
- Mental health issues, including depression and anxiety
- Negative self-talk, including self-deprecating humor

These things occur because by ignoring your shadow self, you are not confronting what is hurting you, instead you are taking the pain out on yourself.

General Guide to Shadow Work

To properly do shadow work, the process starts before you even pick up your pen. By this, I mean that shadow work demands pure honesty. Thankfully, you don't have to talk to anyone else about your shadow, but your honesty has to be with yourself. Good shadow work tackles the concept you have of yourself: Who are you? What do you truly want? What is holding you back?

These are three simple questions, but to get to their answers, you might have to ask yourself an abundance of other questions. I aim to write one to two pages in my journal per question, to truly dig deep for the answer. When you run out of questions, there are always more to answer. My best recommendation is to start by answering one of the following 15 questions per day (Wright, 2022):

- What do I want to get out of shadow work?
- What were my family's values? How do my values line up?
- In what ways am I like my family members? Do I hope to be similar to them or different?
- What cycles or bad habits within my family am I afraid of repeating?
- How would I describe my current life to my child self? What parts of it am I proud to tell them and which am I ashamed of?
- When was the last time I truly felt at peace? What was my environment like? Was I alone or with someone else?
- In what situations do I feel less than, equal to, or better than others?
- What is my definition of failure?
- What do I describe as my biggest personal failure? What caused it?
- When was the last time I was rejected by someone? What did I tell them?
- When was the last time I felt jealous of somebody? What about their success or personality made me feel this way? What do they have that I want?
- When was the last time I felt defensive, and what caused this?
- What behaviors in other people upset me the most? Do I exhibit any of these behaviors myself?

- How forgiving do I tend to be? Am I capable of forgiving others? What would someone have to do that is unforgivable to me?
- How do I treat myself when I do something disappointing or when I fail? Am I kind to myself or do I further beat myself down?

Meditation for the Shadow

If you ever get tired of writing and want to face your shadow directly in your mind, meditation is a wonderful alternative, and a powerful one at that. When I did my first shadow work meditation, I was nearly brought to tears, as I truly started to accept that part of myself. It took several run-throughs over the course of a few weeks for me to be totally at peace with my shadow self, but my work is still not done. You see, our shadows continue to update, re-form, and grow into new incarnations depending on our lives. So, our work with them is never really done.

I would recommend finding a guided meditation for shadow work online. For a lot of them, the guide will encourage you to visualize your shadow as yourself or even as a separate entity. By doing so, you disconnect from it and can interact with it more objectively. All of those self-doubts you harbor are easier to handle when they seem to be coming outside of your regular self.

The guided meditation will likely have you try accepting this version of yourself (or the other entity) for who they are. They might be pessimistic, mean, vengeful, and full of hate, but they still add to who we are. By learning to love this version of yourself, you are telling yourself that you are not ashamed, and don't need to hide who you are.

Talking Through the Hurt

A lot of our shadows are representations of aspects we've absorbed from other people or our interactions with them. We are often unaware of how deeply we are affected by others' words. If we have someone in our lives who brings out the worst in us, we must identify those triggers. In some cases, the people who have hurt us are no longer in our lives for one reason or another, or we simply are unable to talk to them. If this is not the case, however, talking to the person who has deeply hurt you in the past could be an extremely therapeutic process; uncomfortable, yes, but also very freeing.

The following is a guideline for beginning a conversation with someone whom you want to make peace with:

- **Understand your thoughts and feelings.** The last thing you want to do is go into such a tense situation with guns blazing. Ideally, you should have formulated a very clear picture of what exactly you feel and what you want to say.
- **Notify the person.** Each of us has good and bad days, and we need to be respectful of that. Tell the person you want to discuss something important with them and ask when would be a good time for them.
- **Find a neutral environment.** Be mindful of where and when you schedule the conversation, and make sure both of you are comfortable. Find a setting that is comfortable and not too emotional.
- **Express yourself through a three-part statement.** To not trigger the other person's

defensiveness or make them feel attacked, try
expressing yourself as objectively as possible.
Describe what happened, how you felt about it,
and what you think about it now.

Our past shapes who we are; there's no getting around it.
Making peace with our past allows us to truly move
forward; otherwise, you are being actively held back by
what no longer even exists. This includes past people, situations, failures, rejections, and miscalculations. Yes, we can
blame others, but what good would that do if it only makes
us angrier? The entire premise of shadow work is to accept
things for what they are, no matter how uncomfortable that
may be.

Key Points

Let's look over the most important takeaways from
Chapter 10:

- We all have a shadow self—the part of us that
  includes undesirable qualities and attributes
- Accepting and healing your shadow results in
  improved relationships, self-confidence, mental
  clarity, and more
- Journaling and answering shadow work questions
  daily can build your progress up bit by bit
- Meditation is a powerful technique to visualize
  and accept your shadow self
- You can't fix the past, but you should address it,
  especially if somebody has hurt you

Conclusion

There is not a single person who can escape the difficulties caused by negativity. We all struggle, face obstacles, fail, get upset, and sometimes even give up. Success doesn't come easy, but the effort put toward it is worthwhile if what you're working for is truly what you desire. Negativity is no joke and rarely does it ease up on its own. However, through introspection, mindfulness, shadow work, and motivation increase, you can prevent yourself from being swiped down by the avalanche of negativity.

If there is one thing I want you to take away from this book, it's that your negative thoughts should not be your enemies. They exist for a very specific and helpful reason—to help you navigate this crazy world—and it's only when you let them go from insightful guides to overpowering rulers that they become a venom in your life. If those little voices in your head become so deafening that they overshadow all the positive things in your life—including all the things that pose no real threat to you—then it's imperative that you learn to adjust their volume; because, if you try to just tune them out, chances are they will not go away anytime soon.

When your negative thoughts make up the majority of what goes on inside your brain, it's a losing battle to start countering them with positive thoughts, since they will be few and far between at first. The best thing to do is to take the power away from the pre-existing negative thoughts, rather than just conjuring up new, positive ones. For that, you can:

- Look objectively at your negative thoughts and feelings, and accept them without judgment
- Try to get to the bottom of why they appear, what they mean to you, as well as what they mean to your situation
- Let them go gradually, by learning to live with them, but without letting them cause you much pain until eventually they stop coming
- Be kinder to yourself and work on your self-image. None of us are perfect, so don't strive to be
- Improve other areas of your life that will make you a happier person by using various techniques

Remember, you are in control of your inner dialogue, so you must be mindful of what's going on inside your head. By being aware of the path your subconscious might be leading you down, you can change which way you go. You have the power to decide what is true to you, and what you consider to be the most helpful interpretation, at all times.

Positivity is much more unnatural to us than negativity is, so naturally, it will take some extra work for us to become comfortable with it. I promise you, however, that the benefits you reap will prove to be worth it. By making your mind a safe place rather than one of critique and doubting, you begin growing into someone you are not only comfortable being, but are proud of. So, take accountability for your future and don't put off your happiness any longer.

I hope with all my heart that this book was of use to you. Keep in mind that not all of the techniques I shared will resonate with you; it's for this reason that I provided a multitude of various exercises, techniques, and questions to ask yourself so that you can create a method that works just for you. With over a decade of experience, I learned precisely how important it is to try various things out until something sticks.

Thankfully, you won't ever be short of options. Not only do you now have ten chapters of information from me, but countless articles, studies, and educational materials, are being constantly updated online nowadays. With pure intentions and a fiery determination to improve your life, I am confident you will be just fine.

Thank You

Thank you so much for buying my book. I hope it was both informing and insightful.

Before you go, can I ask you for one small favor? **Could you please consider leaving a review on Amazon?**

Your feedback helps independent authors like me to create more books that will hopefully keep on helping you and others.

It would mean the world to me to hear from you.

References

150+ mindfulness quotes to help you live more mindfully. Declutter The Mind. (2021, September 14). Retrieved July 15, 2022, from https://declutterthemind.com/blog/mindfulness-quotes/

175 feel-good happiness quotes: Keep inspiring me. KeepInspiring.me. (2022, June 28). Retrieved July 15, 2022, from https://www.keepinspiring.me/quotes-about-happiness/

44% of students don't know what they want to do after graduation. Concrete. (2015, February 8). Retrieved July 15, 2022, from https://www.concrete-online.co.uk/44-students-dont-know-want-graduation/

Allen, S., & Smith, J. A. (2016). *How happy brains respond to negative things.* Greater Good. Retrieved July 15, 2022, from https://greatergood.berkeley.edu/article/item/how_happy_brains_respond_to_negative_things

Bergeron, L. (2013, November 20). *Size, connectivity of brain region linked to anxiety level in young children, study shows.* News Center. Retrieved July 15, 2022, from https://med.stanford.edu/news/all-news/2013/11/size-connectivity-of-brain-region-linked-to-anxiety-level-in-young-children-study-shows.html

Bloom, L. B. (2022, April 14). *Ranked: The 20 happiest countries in the world in 2022.* Forbes. Retrieved July 15, 2022, from https://www.forbes.com/sites/laurabegleybloom/2022/03/18/ranked-the-20-happiest-countries-in-the-world-in-2022/?sh=5e975d9835d5

Boogaard, K. (2022, February 17). *How to write SMART goals.* Work Life by Atlassian. Retrieved July 15, 2022, from https://www.atlassian.com/blog/productivity/how-to-write-smart-goals

Cherry, K. (2022, May 2). *Which Jungian archetype are you?* Verywell Mind. Retrieved July 15, 2022, from https://www.verywellmind.com/what-are-jungs-4-major-archetypes-2795439#:~:text=The%20shadow%20is%20an%20archetype,to%20cultural%20norms%20and%20expectations.

Clear, J. (2020, February 4). *Inversion: The crucial thinking skill nobody ever taught you.* James Clear. Retrieved July 15, 2022, from https://jamesclear.com/inversion

Congleton, C., Holzel, B. K., & Lazar, S. W. (2021, August 30). *Mindfulness can literally change your brain*. Harvard Business Review. Retrieved July 15, 2022, from https://hbr.org/2015/01/mindfulness-can-literally-change-your-brain#:~:text=Neuroscientists%20have%20also%20shown%20that,thinking%2C%20and%20sense%20of%20self.

Danzico, M. (2011, April 24). *Brains of Buddhist monks scanned in meditation study*. BBC News. Retrieved July 15, 2022, from https://www.bbc.com/news/world-us-canada-12661646

Divorce statistics and facts: What affects divorce rates in the U.S.? Wilkinson & Finkbeiner, LLP. (2022, March 3). Retrieved July 30, 2022, from https://www.wf-lawyers.com/divorce-statistics-and-facts/#:~:text=Almost%2050%20percent%20of%20all,8.

Geggel, L. (2020, March 17). *Meditation may have shaved 8 years of aging off Buddhist monk's brain*. LiveScience. Retrieved July 15, 2022, from https://www.livescience.com/buddhist-monk-meditation-brain.html

Gjersoe, N. (2017, May 26). *Negativity bias: Why Conservatives are more swayed by threats than Liberals*. The Guardian. Retrieved July 15, 2022, from https://www.theguardian.com/science/head-quarters/2017/may/26/negativity-bias-why-conservatives-are-more-swayed-by-threats-than-liberals

Goodreads. (n.d.). *A quote by C.S. Lewis*. Goodreads. Retrieved July 15, 2022, from https://www.goodreads.com/quotes/812245-you-are-never-too-old-to-set-another-goal-or

Goodreads. (n.d.). *A quote by Wayne W. Dyer*. Goodreads. Retrieved July 15, 2022, from https://www.goodreads.com/quotes/126097-what-we-think-determines-what-happens-to-us-so-if

Goodreads. (n.d.). *Overthinking quotes (151 quotes)*. Goodreads. Retrieved July 15, 2022, from https://www.goodreads.com/quotes/tag/overthinking

Goodreads. (n.d.). *Shirley MacLaine quotes (author of out on a limb)*. Goodreads. Retrieved July 15, 2022, from https://www.goodreads.com/author/quotes/63879.Shirley_MacLaine#:~:text=%E2%80%9CDwelling%20on%20the%20nega-tive%20simply%20contributes%20to%20its%20power.%E2%80%9D

Goss, R. (2022, January 26). *This island unlocked the secret to long life-and knows how to get through tough times*. Travel. Retrieved July 15, 2022, from https://www.nationalgeographic.com/travel/article/uncover-the-secrets-of-longevity-in-this-japanese-village

Inspirational quotes about history...and the future. Everyday Power. (2022, July 10). Retrieved July 15, 2022, from https://everydaypower.com/history-quotes/

Inspiring quotes on getting rid of bad habits. Everyday Power. (2022, June 3). Retrieved July 15, 2022, from https://everydaypower.com/quotes-getting-rid-of-bad-habits/

Klemp, N. (2019, August 7). *The neuroscience of breaking out of negative thinking (and how to do it in under 30 seconds).* Inc.com. Retrieved July 15, 2022, from https://www.inc.com/nate-klemp/try-this-neuroscience-based-technique-to-shift-your-mindset-from-negative-to-positive-in-30-seconds.html

Kondo, M. (2014). *The Life-Changing Magic of Tidying up.* Ten Speed Press.

Kondo, M. (2021, August 14). *The joy of sleep, with Arianna Huffington – konmari: The official website of Marie Kondo.* KonMari. Retrieved July 15, 2022, from https://konmari.com/arianna-huffington-sleep/

Lewis, M. (2016, November 14). *How two trailblazing psychologists turned the world of decision science upside down.* Vanity Fair. Retrieved July 15, 2022, from https://www.vanityfair.com/news/2016/11/decision-science-daniel-kahneman-amos-tversky

Mcleod, S. (2020, December 29). *Maslow's hierarchy of needs.* Simply Psychology. Retrieved July 15, 2022, from https://www.simplypsychology.org/maslow.html

Shadow self quotes: Thought-provoking sayings about inner darkness. SOLANCHA. (2020, August 14). Retrieved July 15, 2022, from https://solancha.com/shadow-self-quotes-thought-provoking-sayings-about-inner-darkness/

Tracy, B. (n.d.). *Excerpt from get smart!* Penguin Random House Canada. Retrieved July 15, 2022, from https://www.penguinrandomhouse.ca/books/533286/get-smart-by-brian-tracy/9780399183799/excerpt

Why does your brain love? negativity? the negativity bias. Marbella International University Centre. (2021, June 10). Retrieved July 15, 2022, from https://miuc.org/brain-love-negativity-negativity-bias/#:~:text=Much%20research%20has%20been%20done,known%20to%20cause%20neutral%20feelings.

Wilson, T. D., & Gilbert, D. T. (2005, June 1). *Affective forecasting: Knowing what to want - sage journals.* Sage Journals. Retrieved July 15, 2022, from https://journals.sagepub.com/doi/10.1111/j.0963-7214.2005.00355.x

Wright, J. (2022, January 12). *30 shadow work prompts for healing and growth.* PureWow. Retrieved July 15, 2022, from https://www.purewow.com/wellness/shadow-work-prompts

Xplore. (n.d.). *Aristotle quotes.* BrainyQuote. Retrieved July 15, 2022, from https://www.brainyquote.com/quotes/aristotle_138768

Xplore. (n.d.). *Benjamin Franklin quotes*. BrainyQuote. Retrieved July 15, 2022, from https://www.brainyquote.com/authors/benjamin-franklin-quotes